C000044339

HOME OF HARD-TO-FIND BOOKS

The Spiritual Quixote Or, The Summer"S Ramble of Mr. Geoffry Wildgoose. A Comic Romance

by Unknown

Copyright © 2019 by HardPress

Address:
HardPress
8345 NW 66TH ST #2561
MIAMI FL 33166-2626
USA
Email: info@hardpress.net

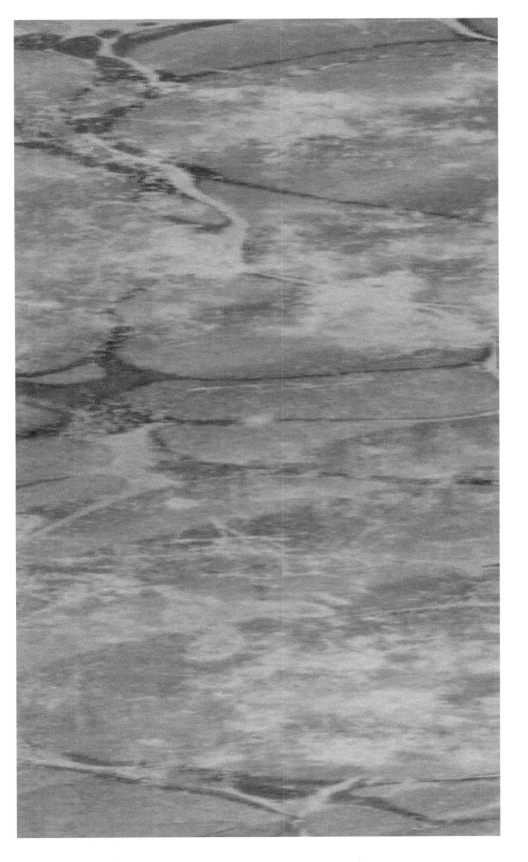

M. Houlbrook

2 0. 726

THE
SPIRITUAL QUIXOTE:
OR, THE
SUMMER'S RAMBLE
OF
Mr. GEOFFRY WILDGOOSE.
A COMIC ROMANCE.

—— multi
Nomine Divorum thalamos iniêre pudicos.

Ov.

— venit & Crispi jucunda senectus.

Juv.

VOL. II.

LONDON:
PRINTED FOR J. DODSLEY, PALL-MALL,
M DCC LXXIII.

BODLEIAN LIBRARY

14
NOV
1928

OXFORD

[v]

CONTENTS

OF
THE SECOND VOLUME.

a 3   CHAP.

C H A P.

a 4 CHAP.

THE

THE
SPIRITUAL QUIXOTE:
OR, THE
SUMMER'S RAMBLE
OF
Mr. GEOFFRY WILDGOOSE.

BOOK V.

CHAP. I.

WHEN the two pilgrims were now
come into the fuburbs of Bath,
Tugwell very civilly enquired which
was the Briſtol road. "Follow your nofe,
"and your a---fe will tag after," fays a
taylor's 'prentice.—"You might learn to be
"more civil to ſtrangers," fays Tugwell,
"for, I am fure, you live by them."—"Not
"by fuch ſtrangers as you," replies the 'prentice; "who preach againſt fine cloaths and in-
"nocent paſtimes."—"Come, come, Maſter,"
fays Jerry, "come along; let us ſhake off

"the duſt of our feet, for a teſtimony againſt
"them."

An elderly man, however, called out to
them, that the way to Briſtol was "ſtraight
"forwards at the firſt turning on the right
"hand." Though this direction was a little
ambiguous, Tugwell was unwilling to hazard
a more minute enquiry: they trudged ſtraight
along therefore, without aſking any further
queſtions.

Tugwell, being highly diſguſted with the
inſolent behaviour of the Bath people, and
expreſſing himſelf with ſome bitterneſs againſt
them; Wildgooſe obſerved, "that the mob of all
" places were alike; and that he ought not to
" reflect upon a whole body of people, for the
" wanton petulance of a few ignorant wretches."

Jerry then aſked what my landlord had
charged for his ſupper at Bath.   "Why,
" only eight-pence a night," ſays Wildgooſe.
" Eight-pence a night!" ſays Jerry;   " an
" unconſcionable, diſtorting raſcal! why, I
" will be hanged if I have eat three penny-
" worth of bread and cheeſe for ſupper the
" three nights that we have been there. I have
" a good mind to go and make the rogue give
" me back your Worſhip's money."—" No,
                                    " no,

" no, Jerry, thefe things are cuftomary; and
" it is beft to pay it without making a di-
" fturbance. At thefe houfes, one pays for
" lodging, and houfe-room, and attendance,
" as well as merely for what one eats and
" drinks; and I think, upon the whole, we
" came off very reafonably."

Thus they went on talking near two miles;
and, having reached the fummit of the hills
when it drew towards evening, they came to
a place where the roads divided. Mr. Wildgoofe was inclined to turn to the right, and
Tugwell to the left hand; which created a
little debate upon the probability of each opinion. But Tugwell, having learnt to decide
dubious points by lot, threw up an half-penny,
crying out, " that heads fhould determine him
" to the right, and tails to the left hand road."
Fortune declared for the former; which Jerry,
then changing his note, faid *muft* be the road
to Briftol, by the *courfe* of the country.

While they were yet debating the affair,
Tugwell, fpying a man in a plain drap coat
walking foberly at a fmall diftance from the
road, calls out, " Holloo! Mafter! Mafter!
" which is the road to Briftol?" Whether the
gentleman was immerfed in thought, or whe-

B 2   ther

ther he difliked the familiarity of Jerry's com-
pellation, he made no anfwer. Wildgoofe
therefore, advancing a little towards him, repeated the queftion in a more civilized manner,
and afked which of thofe two was the road to
Briftol. "Why, neither of them," replied
the gentleman; "the road you are in would
"lead you to Wells." Wildgoofe was going
to crave his affiftance, to put him in the right
way; when he and the ftranger furveying each
other with an air of furprife, "What! Mr.
"Rivers!" cries Wildgoofe.—"Blefs my foul!
"my friend Wildgoofe!" replies he; "what
"expedition can you poffibly be upon in this
"part of the world?" They then embraced
(in the language of Romance) or, in plain
Englifh, took each other by the hand with
great cordiality, expreffing great joy at this unexpected rencounter: for they had been very
intimate in the univerfity, though no fort of intercourfe had paft between them for fix or feven
years.

Wildgoofe enquired how long he had been
in this country, and whether he was fettled
any where in the neighbourhood, as he knew
him to be originally a north-country man.
Mr. Rivers told him, he had an houfe within a
mile

mile of that place; whither he infifted upon Wildgoofe's accompanying him for that night at leaft, as it was now too late to go to Briftol on foot, if they had not been fome miles out of their road. Wildgoofe and his companion were well enough pleafed with the invitation, in their prefent circumftances: befides, as Wildgoofe recollected that Mr. Rivers had in his youth a very religious turn, and that was always uppermoft in his thoughts, he immediately conceived fome hopes of converting his old friend to his own opinions. As they went along, Mr. Wildgoofe, at Rivers's requeft, let him into the nature of his prefent undertaking; at which his friend expreffed fome concern, as well as the greateft aftonifhment; but politely added, " that he was glad even of this opportunity of " renewing their friendfhip."

CHAP.

CHAP. II.

Description of Mr. Rivers's House, and some Account of his present Situation.

MR. Rivers had now brought his friend Wildgoose, with Tugwell, to the brow of the hill, which overlooked one of those rich vallies in which that part of the country abounds. A gate opened into a wood, through which they descended, by a rough, unfrequented road,

" Where the gilt chariot never mark'd the way," almost to the bottom of the hill. There an old Gothic mansion presented itself, surrounded towards the road by a lofty stone-wall, covered with moss, maiden-hair, and other wild plants, enough to puzzle the whole Royal Society, and the indefatigable Dr. Hill into the bargain. The house seemed to have been built during the civil wars between the houses of York and Lancaster ; but had been *modernized* in Queen Elizabeth's reign, and new-glazed and painted for the reception of Mr. Rivers.

Rivers knocked at the gate ; which being opened by a servant in a russet coat, they now came

came into an elegant court, where they were regaled with the fight and fragrance of all the flowers of the feafon. From thence they entered a gloomy old-fafhioned hall, but neatly fitted up; the wall covered with maps and chronological tables, above which were a number of cheap prints, reprefenting the cuftoms and habits of the various nations of the world.

Mr. Rivers then, fhewing Tugwell with his wallet the way towards the kitchen, took his friend Wildgoofe into a large wainfcotted parlour, adorned with fome fine prints, a few good paintings, and a buft or two over the chimney: but all his attention was immediately fixed upon Mrs. Rivers, to whom his friend introduced him. She was fitting (like the divinity of the place) at the upper end of the room, at her needle, attended by a boy, and a fine girl about five or fix years old. Mrs. Rivers received Wildgoofe, as her hufband's friend, with a fweet fmile; which, like the fun-fhine fo much admired in the landfchapes of Claude Lorraine, diffufed an additional chearfulnefs over every other object.

Mrs. Rivers was about five and twenty, tall, and well-fhaped; and though the pleafing cares

of

of a young family had taken off a little of her
firſt bloom, yet had it given ſuch a languiſhing
air to her eyes, and ſuch a delicacy to her
complexion, as rather improved than dimi-
niſhed her charms.

Mr. Rivers informed her who Mr. Wildgooſe
was, and how accidentally they had met. She
made ſome obliging ſpeech upon the occaſion,
and then rang the bell for tea; which being
over, Mr. and Mrs. Rivers attended Mr. Wildgooſe into a garden, which commanded a beautiful, though confined, proſpect. It was laid
out in a romantic taſte, with a proper mixture
of the allegro and the penſeroſo, the chearful
and the gloomy: tufts of roſes, jaſmines, and
the moſt fragrant flowering ſhrubs, with a ſer-
pentine walk of cypreſſes and laurels, here and
there an urn, with ſuitable inſcriptions, and
terminated by a rough arch of rock-work that
covered a dripping fountain, were its principal beauties.

After a few turns, Mrs. Rivers being ſum-
moned by her maid to a conſultation about ſupper, Wildgooſe, notwithſtanding his religious
ſeverity, made ſome encomiums upon her perſon and behaviour, and ſaid, " he was leſs ſur-
priſed at his friend's marrying ſo early in life,
than.

than at his good fortune in meeting with so agreeable a woman." He expressed some desire, therefore, to be informed of the particular incidents of Mr. Rivers's life since he left the university. "Why, says he, though my story has nothing very uncommon in it, yet, as I flatter myself that I have escaped into one of the fortunate islands, from that rock on which the happiness of many a young fellow is totally ship-wrecked, I think, as an experienced voyager, I ought to satisfy the curiosity of a friend, and give him all the intelligence in my power, that he may steer the like course with equal success." Then, taking Wildgoose into an alcove, shaded with honey-suckles and sweet-briars, Rivers thus began his narration.

C H A P.   III.

The History of Mr. Rivers and Charlotte Woodville.

"SOON after you left the university," says Mr. Rivers, "I was elected fellow of a "very worthy society, where I pursued my stu-"dies with some regularity, and spent near "two years greatly to my satisfaction: but,

B 5 "whether

" whether the way of life was too sedentary,
" or too sociable, (for I usually spent the day
" in reading, and the evening in company)
" whatever was the cause, I found myself after
" some time in a very indifferent state of health.
" I determined therefore, during the long va-
" cation, to retire into the country. But, as
" I had neither father nor mother living, and
" my fellowship obliged me to an occasional resi-
" dence, I did not care to travel into ——shire,
" which, you know, is my native country, and
" where I had an elder brother and some near
" relations residing ; but was recommended by
" an acquaintance to a pleasant village in
" ——shire, about twenty miles from Oxford ;
" who also prevailed upon a gentleman farmer,
" of whom he had some knowledge, to take me as
" a boarder.

" Mr. Woodville, which was the farmer's
" name, was a very worthy, honest man, and
" had a spirit of generosity far above his situa-
" tion. He was, indeed, quite a gentleman, in
" his appearance, behaviour, and way of think-
" ing. He was about fifty, and had married
" for his first wife a young lady of a genteel
" family, by whom he had one son and two
" daughters : but, being afterwards almost a
" cripple

" cripple with a rheumatic gout, he had been
" perfuaded to marry a good motherly fort of
" woman, beneath his own circumftances;
" who was glad of the match, (though fure to be
" a nurfe) for the fake of providing better for
" her children by a former hufband.

" I had here a tolerable apartment, entirely di-
" ftinct from the reft of the family; which fuited
" with my fcheme of profecuting my ftudies,
" and of giving a particular attention to my
" health, which was the principal end of my
" retiring from college; having, as you know,
" little tafte for the more robuft diverfions of the
" country. But, in this retreat, remote as I
" was from the intrufion of my former jovial
" affociates, I did not long enjoy an abfolute
" tranquillity.

" There are few perfons of fo phlegmatic a
" conftitution as to content themfelves with
" merely rational purfuits. The paffions, the
" appetites, and the imagination, all lay claim
" to their refpective gratifications. Love par-
" ticularly is a plant which fprings up fo na-
" turally in the breafts of young people, that,
" when I hear one in the heat of youth affect
" to talk with a ftoical indifference of that
" tender paffion, I generally fufpect him of

B 6   " indulging

" indulging it privately, either for an *unworthy*,
" or at leaft for an *improper* objeƈt. The
" latter only was my cafe; for though an en-
" gagement of that kind was highly *improper*
" in my circumftances, yet the objeƈt itfelf
" was worthy the love, I might fay the am-
" bition, of a prince.

" Mr. Woodville, as I have faid, had two
" daughters. The elder was about nineteen ;
" and though fhe had nothing remarkably de-
" feƈtive in her features, yet the four and
" felfifh paffions had taken fuch abfolute pof-
" feffion of her countenance, as to render her
" almoft ugly. The younger daughter was
" hardly fifteen, and as different from the elder
" as a Grace from a Fury.

" Defcriptions of a beloved objeƈt are gene-
" rally heightened, and ufually embellifhed
" with all the charms which the enraptured
" imagination is able to give them. Charlotte
" Woodville however was, I think, fo near
" perfeƈtion in that refpeƈt, that, although a
" fevere critic might poffibly fpy out fome
" trifling defeƈt, yet, upon the whole, fhe had
" fo ftriking an appearance, that few people
" could behold her without admiration.

" She

" She was rather tall than of a middling
ftature, but every way finely proportioned,
and of a natural, eafy fhape. Her features
were neither too large, nor too fmall; the
extremes in either refpect being, I think,
lefs agreeable. Her eyes had always fuch a
brilliant luftre, that I never knew their real
colour. But her hair (which fhe had in great
abundance) was of a bright brown, and
gave an inimitably fine fhade to her complexion. Her complection had, at that time,
rather the gloffy bloom of high health, than
that tranfparent delicacy which is generally
the concomitant of too tender a conftitution.

" But, what gave the greateft fpirit and
force to her external charms, was the beauty
of her mind, which was every thing that can
be conceived of fweet and amiable. Good-
nature and good fenfe, fprightlinefs and an
artlefs freedom, the emanations of her
charming foul, diftinguifhed themfelves in
her eyes, and in every feature of her face.

" Such was this young creature in her native fimplicity, without the leaft affiftance of
art, or indeed of any other education, than
what was to be met with in a country place;
and which the lofs of a genteel mother, when

" fhe

" she was very young, had not suffered to be
" applied to the utmoſt advantage."

" Sir," ſays Wildgooſe ſmiling, " you might
" have ſpared yourſelf the trouble, or rather
" denied yourſelf the pleaſure, of this deſcrip-
" tion; for, in the picture you have drawn, I
" can eaſily diſcover the features of Mrs. Ri-
" vers, though a few years may have abated, or
" rather ſoftened, the glaring luſtre of the co-
" louring. But proceed, my friend, in your
" narration."

" Well," ſays Rivers, " you may ſuppoſe
" a young fellow, though of more philoſophy
" than ever I pretended to, could not be long
" in the ſame family, without taking particular
" notice of ſo lovely an object. But, as any
" ſort of love-engagement would have been
" highly improper in my circumſtances, a
" diſcreet perſon would certainly have checked
" any tender ſentiments, and not have thought
" of trifling with ſo young a creature, who,
" conſidering my education and future pro-
" ſpects in life, was, in a *prudential* view, be-
" neath my conſideration. For, according to
" the maxims of the world,

" Love's but the frailty of the mind,
" When 'tis not with ambition join'd."

" Ah !"

" Ah !" says Wildgoose, " nothing but
" the love of God can satisfy the *reasonable am-*
" *bition* of an immortal soul."—" Well," replies Rivers, " every man to his taste. But
" to proceed in my story."

C H A P. IV.

Mr. Rivers's and Charlotte Woodville's Story
continued.

" A S I was at that time quite a valetudina-
" rian, and willing also to lose as little
" time as possible from my studies, I desired to
" eat at my own hours, and avoided all inter-
" course with the family as much as I decently
" could without the appearance of pride or
" moroseness. Mrs. Woodville kept one maid
" to do the work within doors; and whose
" business it was to wait upon me : but, as she
" was often otherwise engaged, the daughters
" would frequently by turns supply her place.
" After some time, however, I could not but
" observe, that the younger was more assiduous
" in her attendance on me than the elder ;
" which yet I looked upon as accidental, and
2   " imputed

" imputed it either to the good-nature of the
" one, or the churlish temper of the other.
" Charlotte Woodville did every thing in so
" pretty a manner, that although it gave me
" no small pleasure, yet was it a somewhat
" painful tax upon my complaisance, which
" would not suffer me to receive any thing
" from so fair a hand without some little
" gallant acknowledgment. The more civi-
" lity I shewed, the more obliging was this
" fair nymph ; so that by degrees, as I seemed
" disappointed whenever any other part of the
" family attended me, so she grew more kindly
" officious in her attendance, and,

" Tho' I call'd another, Charlotte came *.

" I am convinced, however, that she was ut-
" terly void of any design in this, and at pre-
" sent only followed the dictates of her na-
" tive benevolence and freedom of disposi-
" tion : though a more powerful motive, I
" believe, soon took place in her little breast ;
" and *my* indiscretion put matters upon a dif-
" ferent footing.

" There happened to be a wedding in the
" village one morning ; and curiosity had
" drawn to church the whole family except

* Prior.

" the

" the younger daughter, who ſtaid to attend
" on her father, who was confined to his bed by
" a fit of the gout. Charlotte came into the
" parlour, upon ſome occaſion or other, while
" the bells were ringing upon this jocund
" occaſion. A wedding in a country place
" ſets every girl in the pariſh to ſimpering;
" and, matrimony being an inexhauſtible
" topick of raillery, I happened to joke with
" Charlotte upon the happineſs of the ſtate.
" She made me ſome very innocent reply;
" which however tempted me to chuck her
" under the chin, the loweſt degree of dal-
" liance with an inferior. She bluſhed, and
" retired with ſome precipitation, and with
" ſuch a ſweet confuſion, that I longed to re-
" peat the freedom; and begging her to re-
" turn for a moment, as ſoon as ſhe came
" within the door, I caught her round the
" neck, and ſnatched a kiſs. This increaſed
" her ſurprize, and ſhe again retired with a
" glow upon her cheeks, which I fancied ex-
" preſſed ſome indignation; at leaſt it ſo
" alarmed her virgin innocence, that I ſaw
" her no more that day.

" I had now paſſed the rubicon of diſcre-
" tion."—" Yes," ſays Wildgooſe, " you had
" taſted

" tafted the forbidden fruit. ' The poifon of
" afps is under the lips' of the moft inno-
" cent of the fex. There is no fecurity againft
" the encroachments of love, but by check-
" ing the firft motions of the foul. ' Whofo
" looketh upon a woman, to luft after her,
" has committed adultery already with her in
" his heart."

" You are too fevere upon me," replied
Rivers ; " but I will proceed in my narration."

C H A P. V.

The Story continued.

" I TOOK a walk before dinner; and,
" upon my return through the hall, where
" the family generally fate, Charlotte, inftead
" of meeting my eyes with an open, chearful
" countenance, looked down with a bafhful
" confcioufnefs, and almoft hid her face in her
" bofom.

" My mind was now in fuch a fituation,
" that, if I had believed the freedom which
" I took had really offended this innocent
" maid, I fhould probably have entirely de-
" fifted, and have purfued the affair no fur-
" ther : but, as a little coldnefs would eafily

" have

" have nipped my paffion in the bud, fo the
" flighteft encouragement fufficed to keep alive
" the flame. I cannot omit a trifling circum-
" ftance, which I confidered in that light.

" Being under a kind of regimen as to my
" diet, I ufually fupped upon a bafon of milk.
" This the fervant brought me that evening,
" accompanied with a plate of wood-ftraw-
" berries. It being early in the year, I afked
" her whence they came. She faid, they were
" a prefent to one of her young miftreffes.
" As I had met with fo little complaifance
" from the elder, I eafily gueffed to whom I
" was obliged for this favour. This flight
" inftance of her forgivenefs, expreffed in fo
" pretty a manner, tended but little to the
" cure of my growing paffion.

" The next day, in the abfence of the maid,
" Charlotte ventured again into my apartment.
" I gave her a fignificant fmile, in allufion to
" what had paffed the day before; and, taking
" her hand, preffed it with fome eagernefs.
" She repulfed me in fuch a manner, as feemed
" rather to return the compliment, than to be
" difpleafed with it. In fhort, though I had
" no great opinion of my own perfon, yet I be-
" gan to flatter myfelf that I had made fome
                                    " little

" little impreffion upon Charlotte's tender
" heart : and, as nothing is a ftronger incen-
" tive to love than an opinion of its being
" mutual, this naturally endeared her to me,
" and made her appear more amiable every
" time I faw her. In reality, I began to love
" her extravagantly.

" And fhe more lovely grew, as more belov'd.

" Jealoufy is often a fign of a little mind and
" a meannefs of fpirit; and a jealous *hufband*
" is certainly a ridiculous animal : but a jea-
" lous *lover*, I think, deferves the compaffion,
" rather than the contempt, of his miftrefs.
" Sufpicion after marriage betrays a want of
" confidence in her of whofe fidelity we are
" fuppofed to have received fufficient affurance.
" But it is excufable in a lover to be a little
" apprehenfive of the fuccefs of his rival, when
" it would be efteemed a degree of prefumption
" to be too confident of his own preference in
" her affection and efteem. In fhort, what-
" ever a woman may think of a jealous lover
" in other refpects, fhe can have no reafon
" to doubt of the fincerity of his paffion.

" For my part, I began to be fo fond of my
" little miftrefs, that I could hardly fuffer her
" to be out of my fight; and, as I thought
                                        " I had

" I had condefcended a little in fettling my
" affections, I could not bear with patience
" the thoughts of a rival ; nor, indeed, had I
" any reafon to fear one in her prefent fitua-
" tion. However, I one evening faw her
" engaged in fo fprightly a converfation, and
" laughing with fo coquettifh an air (as I fan-
" cied) with a young fellow of the neighbour-
" hood, who was talking to her brother at the
" door, that it immediately alarmed my jea-
" loufy, and I could not forbear difcovering
" it. I rang the bell with fome vehemence,
" intending only to put her in mind of me.
" Inftead of fending the maid, as I expected,
" fhe immediately left her company, and came
" herfelf. I bid her fend in a glafs of water,
" which, with great good-nature, fhe brought
" with her own hands. I had feated myfelf,
" fultan-like, in a great chair ; and, loiling
" in an infolent pofture, affected to be engaged
" in reading, and with a haughty nod bid her
" fet it down. She was fenfible of the infult,
" and, immediately affuming the dignity of her
" fex, drew herfelf up, and flung out of the
" room with the air of a countefs.

" It appeared afterwards, indeed, that the
" young man, whom I feared as a rival, was
" at

" at, this time engaged, and upon the brink of
" being married, to another girl in the neigh-
" bourhood; and I was convinced, that my fuf-
" picions with regard to Charlotte were entirely
" without the leaft foundation. The little
" quarrels of lovers generally conclude in more
" tender reconciliations. Mifs Woodville's fpi-
" rited behaviour on this occafion, and the ex-
" planation which it produced, greatly aug-
" mented our fondnefs for each other; and this
" tender intercourfe was continued for fome
" time, without being fufpected by any one.
" I was fo happy in my amour, that I never
" confidered the probable confequences of fo
" improper an engagement, but rather fhut my
" eyes againft any difagreeable reflections.

" As a French writer * obferves, ' The
" moft common view that people have, when
" they commit imprudent actions, is the *poffi-*
" *bility* of finding out always fome refource
" or other:' fo I flattered myfelf with the
" notion of being able to recall my affections
" when I thought it proper; and imagined I
" might amufe myfelf for fome time, inno-
" cently enough, in fo retired a place, without
" fubjecting myfelf to the cenfure or re-

* Card. de Retz.

" marks

" marks of any one, whofe opinion I much
" regarded."

CHAP. VI.

The Story continued.

" ABOUT this time I thought it ne-
" ceffary to vifit my friends in Stafford-
" fhire, being particularly invited by an old
" relation, whom you have heard me mention,
" the little fat clergyman, from whom I have
" always had fome confiderable expectations.
" Though I found myfelf at prefent but little
" inclined to take fuch a journey; yet I had
" fixed the day, which was now at hand.

" As my interviews with Mifs Woodville
" had hitherto been very tranfient, and there
" was no probability of our ever being long
" together without fubjecting ourfelves to
" obfervation, I made a requeft to her, in
" which I was afraid fhe could not oblige me;
" and that was, to give me an hour of her com-
" pany in the evening, after the family were
" in bed. As Mifs Woodville was very young
" and innocent, and entirely ignorant of the
" arts of our fex, having never had any female
" friend to caution her againft them, fhe made

" no

" no fcruple of promifing me her company, if
" fhe could get her fifter (who was drowfily
" enough inclined) to fleep without her; in or-
" der to which, fhe would fit up in her cham-
" ber, fhe faid, under pretence of finifhing fome
" piece of needle-work, which fhe was very
" intent upon.

" When night came, and the family were
" retired, I fate myfelf down, with great com-
" pofure, to wait the event of our affigna-
" tion: I even took a book, and read, (to
" amufe my impatience) but with as little at-
" tention as our candidates for a degree read
" their wall-lectures, when they expect the
" beadle every moment with the joyful news
" that their time is expired. Thus I waited
" for near two hours, and now quite defpaired
" of my promifed happinefs; when, unex-
" pectedly, the ftillnefs of the night was agree-
" ably interrupted by a gentle rap at the par-
" lour-door. I ftarted up, and opened it with
" great alacrity. In fhe came, but with a
" down-caft look, and fweet blufh upon her
" countenance, and with an apology for the
" rafhnefs of her conduct, which her native
" modefty now reprefented to her in the
" ftrongeft light.

" I told

" I told her, 'I had begun to defpair of be-
" ing favoured with her company, and afked
" her if her fifter had any fufpicion of her in-
" tention.—— ' I believe not,' fays Charlotte,
" for fhe was afleep in five minutes after fhe
" was in bed.'—' Why then did you delay my
" happinefs fo long?' faid I. She replied,
" ' That, upon thinking better of it, fhe was
" afraid fhe had done wrong in promifing me,
" and had more than once refolved not to come
" down; nay, that fhe had actually been in
" bed, but as I talked of going early in the
" morning, fhe had not the heart to difap-
" point me.'—' I acknowledged her goodnefs,
" and affured her, 'fhe fhould never repent of
" the confidence fhe repofed in me.'

" I could not but take notice of one particu-
" larity in Mifs Woodville's conduct on this
" occafion; which was, that fhe had taken
" the pains to put on a clean apron, hand-
" kerchief, and ruffles, and adjufted every part
" of her drefs with the niceft exactnefs; which
" trifling circumftance convinced me both of
" the delicacy of her tafte, and the purity of
" her imagination, or rather that fhe was ab-
" folutely void of 'the leaft apprehenfion of any

Vol. II.   C   " thing

" thing contrary to the ſtricteſt decency in
" my behaviour to her.

" Nothing can be more inſipid, upon repe-
" tition, than the converſation of two fond lo-
" vers ; and it is a ſort of prophanation to re-
" peat any thing that paſſes upon thoſe occa-
" ſions : but, as ſomething very ſerious enſued
" from this interview, I cannot forbear men-
" tioning a few trifling particulars. I kept
" her up pretty late. My journey and the
" month's abſence was the principal ſubject
" of our converſation ; in the courſe of
" which ſhe expreſſed her apprehenſion, ' that
" there were probably more ladies which
" I was fond of in other places.'—' Oh ! what
" is life without love ?' ſaid I ? ' To be ſure, I
" muſt have a miſtreſs at every place I go to ;
" half a *dozen* at Oxford, you may ſuppoſe.'
" She affected a ſort of laugh at the humour of
" my deſcriptions, and, I imagined, took it, as
" I deſigned it, merely as unmeaning chit-chat.
" ' But my favourite girl, continued I, is a
" ————ſhire laſs, the very picture of yourſelf,
" a tall, brown beauty, and the beſt-tempered
" creature in the world. O ! how happy ſhall
" I be next Thurſday night !' ¡

" Nothing

" Nothing can equal my aftonifhment at
" what now happened. Whilft I was run-
" ning on in this coxcomical ftrain, I found
" her funk back in her chair, pale as death,
" without breath or motion, or the leaft ap-
" pearance of life. I was fhocked, and di-
" ftreffed to the laft degree how to proceed.
" I could not bring myfelf to alarm the fa-
" mily, and yet had the moft terrible appre-
" henfions of what might be the event of this
" affair.

" There was a decanter of water ftood on
" the table, fome of which I fprinkled in her
" face ; and having fome fpirit of lavender in
" my pocket, I rubbed her temples with that,
" and applied fome to her noftrils ; which, af-
" ter a few minutes, very happily brought her
" to herfelf again.

" I curfed my own folly, and affured her,
" ' that what I had faid was a mere jeft, and
" that there was not a girl in the world for
" whom I had the leaft fondnefs, but herfelf.'

" This proof of Mifs Woodville's affection
" for me, you may be fure, endeared her to
" me extremely ; and I parted from her the next
" morning with the greateft reluctance.

C 2 CHAP.

CHAP. VII.

The Story continued.

" I HAD proposed being out a month on my
" journey; but my eager desire to see my
" fair villager made me shorten my absence,
" and I returned in less than three weeks.

" As I had written to Mr. Woodville, and
" given him notice of my intention, I found
" every thing in great order for my reception;
" but was disappointed in not finding Charlotte
" Woodville ready to welcome me on my ar-
" rival : the rest of the family were sitting in
" their usual apartment. After making my com-
" pliments to him, I *affected* to look round, and
" enquired if some part of the family were
" not wanting. Mr. Woodville looked down
" with some confusion; but Mrs. Woodville,
" affecting a smile, answered, ' that their
" daughter Charlotte was gone to school again
" for a little time; that, as she discovered a
" tolerable hand at her needle, they were
" willing to improve her as much as possible :
" she will be at home again in the evening,'
" continued she, and then turned the discourse.
" I imme-

" I immediately suspected there was some
" mystery in this, as I had often heard her ex-
" tolled for her extraordinary skill in needle-
" work, and was convinced she could not learn
" much at the place they mentioned, which
" was at the next village, whither I found she
" was forced to walk every morning, and return
" in the evening: besides, I knew it must be a
" great mortification to a girl of Charlotte's
" spirit (who was near fifteen, and very tall of
" her age) to be sent to such a paltry school
" amongst a parcel of children.

" I waited with great impatience for the
" evening and Charlotte Woodville's return.
" At last I heard her voice in the next room;
" which was musick to my ears. I immedi-
" ately ran towards the door, where I could
" hear every thing that passed. Poor Char-
" lotte, seeing some unusual preparations
" for supper, enquired into the occasion of
" them. ' Oh!' says the step-mother, ' I sup-
" pose you can give a shrewd guess. It is for
" you and your gentleman, I suppose, after
" we *are in bed*.' This spiteful speech of the
" old lady let me a little into the secret, and
" soon convinced me that our intimacy was
" discovered.

C 3

" As

"As I imagined therefore I should have no
"other opportunity of seeing or speaking to
"her that evening, I immediately went out
"into the room where the family was, under
"pretence of enquiring how long it was to
"supper. The moment Charlotte saw me, a
"blush overspread her cheeks; which was
"succeeded by a total want of colour. She
"just courtesied, and welcomed me home;
"when she was dispatched by the old lady,
"upon some frivolous pretence or other, into
"another room; and I saw her no more that
"evening.

"The next morning, however, we found
"an opportunity of being alone together for
"a few minutes; when Miss Charlotte in-
"formed me of the true situation of our af-
"fairs. She said, 'That her sister, having
"some suspicion of my affection for her, had
"feigned herself asleep the night when she came
"down to me, and had discovered it to her
"father and mother; that her father had given
"her a very serious lecture upon the occasion;
"but that her mother-in-law had been out-
"rageous about it, had talked at first of desiring
"me to quit my lodgings immediately, to
"which her father would not consent, he
                                    "having

" having expreſſed a great opinion of my ho-
" nour and of my innocent intentions; in
" ſhort, that at laſt they had come to a de-
" termination to ſend her out to ſchool for the
" preſent, till they could think of ſome other
" way of diſpoſing of her.'

" Any one might imagine from this, that
" Mrs. Woodville was a very careful ſtep-
" mother, and had the true intereſt of her
" huſband's children greatly at heart. But
" the reverſe of this was really the caſe. She
" was what might be called, on the whole,
" a good ſort of woman : but in all ſecond
" marriages, if there are children on both ſides,
" there muſt neceſſarily be ſeparate intereſts ;
" and a woman, who had changed her ſtate
" with that view, could not be much blamed
" for conſulting chiefly the good of her own
" offspring. But, in order to do that effectu-
" ally, another point muſt be ſecured ; I mean,
" an abſolute ſovereignty over her huſband's
" affections ; which Mrs. Woodville ſeemed
" to have gained, and of which ſhe was ex-
" ceſſively jealous. As Charlotte Woodville
" then was deſervedly a favourite with her
" father, no wonder that the mother-in-law
" took every opportunity of leſſening her in his

C 4

" eſteem

" esteem, and even desired to wean his affection
" from the darling of his age. She was pleased
" therefore with this instance of her indiscre-
" tion, which she aggravated to the highest
" degree. She said, ' it confirmed what she
" had often insinuated to him, that Charlotte
" was a proud and forward hussey ;' and insulted
" him with the prudent behaviour of her elder
" sister, who, for an obvious reason, had
" never been guilty of any thing of this kind.
" Mrs. Woodville had really no more regard
" for the elder daughter than the other : but,
" as Miss Betsy's unhappy temper made her
" no great favourite with the rest of the family,
" Mrs. Woodville, by a very slender shew of
" kindness, had bribed her to her interest, and
" employed her as a sort of spy upon her sister ;
" which office she executed with an ill-natured
" fidelity, not scrupling sometimes to exceed
" the bounds of veracity, in order to ingratiate
" herself with her constituent.

" For old Mrs. Woodville not only consi-
" dered her daughter Charlotte as a rival in her
" husband's affections ; but also envied her the
" probability of so advantageous a match as
" mine was considered to be, and could not
" bear the thoughts of her being treated by me
　　　　　　　　　　　　　　　　" with

" with such distinction. She therefore took
" every opportunity of mortifying her; and,
" in order to lessen her consequence in my eyes,
" put her upon any servile employment in the
" family for which she could find a decent ex-
" cuse. In short, though she contrived to
" make poor Charlotte's situation (and mine
" upon her account) as disagreeable as an
" excessive spleen, joined with absolute power,
" could do, yet her behaviour had a contrary
" effect from what she expected, and only the
" more endeared to me the innocent object of
" her persecution.

" Accordingly, I found my passion for this
" young creature daily increase; and we con-
" tinued our intimacy for some time. I had,
" indeed, indulged my fondness the more freely,
" as I fancied myself entirely retired from, and
" unnoticed by, the world; but in this I was
" greatly mistaken.

C 5

CHAP.

CHAP. VIII.

The Story continued.

" IT is more difficult for a man to live *incognito*
" in a country village than in the moſt po-
" pulous city. The very precautions he takes
" to conceal himſelf alarm the curioſity of the
" neighbourhood; and as, in a retired place,
" ſmall matters ſerve for amuſement, the moſt
" trifling incidents ſoon become the ſubject of
" general converſation.

" As my regard for Miſs Woodville was
" now no longer a ſecret in the family, it
" ſoon ſpread through the neighbourhood;
" and by ſome means or other the news had
" been conveyed to my friends in the univer-
" ſity. Accordingly, the next time I went
" thither, I was attacked on all ſides, and
" raillied with great freedom, upon the ſubject
" of my amour: nay, one of my more inti-
" mate friends, when we were alone together,
" took upon him with great ſeriouſneſs to ex-
" poſtulate with me about the imprudence of
" it. He repreſented the ill conſequences of
" ſuch

" such early engagements, and the inconve-
" niences of fettling in life without a proper
" competency, in fuch glowing colours, and
" fet the cruelty of involving a young girl,
" that I had an affection for, in the diftrefs of
" narrow circumftances, in fo ftrong a light;
" and, in fhort, he harangued upon thefe to-
" pics fo long, that at laft I told him, ' I was
" refolved to break off all correfpondence,
" with her, and, in order to that, to quit my
" fituation in Buckinghamfhire as foon as I
" conveniently could.'—' Well, then,' fays my
" friend, taking me at my word, ' I will ride
" over, and fettle your affairs there to-morrow
" morning, and make fome excufe for your
" fudden decampment.'—Here I found my re-
" folution begin to ftagger. Charlotte had
" taken fuch poffeffion of my heart, that I
" could not bear the thoughts of being ba-
" nifhed from her for ever. I haftily inter-
" rupted my officious counfellor, and told
" him, ' that my affairs were in fuch a fituation
" there, that I muft neceffarily go over *once*
" *more* myfelf; but, however, that I would
" (if poffible) take fome opportunity of break-
" ing off my imprudent engagement.' He flew
" into a violent paffion, and immediately gave

C 6   " me

" me up for loft. ' Then' fays he, ' will
" this little flut, with one falfe tear, [*und*
" *falsâ lacrymalâ quam vix vi exprefferit*]
" undo all that I have been labouring;' and,
" having faid this, he left me with an empha-
" tical fhake of the head, and a fmile, which
" expreffed both indignation and contempt.

" However, I returned into Buckinghamfhire
" the next day, full of philofophical reflections,
" and abfolutely determined (as I flattered
" myfelf) to regulate with prudence at leaft,
" if not to put an end to, this imprudent
" amour. But it is very difficult to know
" one's own heart; and, whenever reafon pre-
" vails over paffion, it is more frequently, I
" believe, to be attributed to the weaknefs of
" the one, than to the ftrength of the other.
" The moment I faw Mifs Woodville, I
" found my refolution begin to fail me; and
" though I was weak enough to inform her
" of what had paffed at Oxford, and even of
" the defign I had formed of leaving her for
" fome time, till I had finifhed my ftudies,
" and was in fuch circumftances as might make
" it more prudent for us to come together, yet
" I found my project fo inconfiftent with the
" prefent fituation of my heart, and the pro-
" 　　　　　　　　　　　　　　　　　" feffions

3

" feſſions I had hitherto made, that I was heart-
" ily aſhamed of the figure I muſt make in this.
" young creature's eyes. And, as an unſuc-
" ceſsful rebellion ſtrengthens the hands of
" the government, ſo this temporary defection.
" from my duty helped to rivet my chains;
" and our interview ended, on my part, with.
" more earneſt proteſtations of future fidelity,.
" and a ſolemn promiſe never to forſake her.

C H A P. IX.

The Story continued.

" THOUGH Miſs Woodville and I be-
"   haved with great caution and reſerve to
" each other in the family, ſo as not to give
" Mrs. Woodville an opportunity of any open.
" expoſtulation with us upon the ſubject ; yet,
" ſhe was ſo provoked at the ſucceſs (as ſhe
" eſteemed it) of her daughter-in-law's charms,
" that, with pretended concern for her daugh-
" ter's reputation, ſhe privately inſiſted upon
" Mr. Woodville's talking to me upon it, and
" bringing me to an explanation. He took an
" occaſion, one day when I was alone with
                                              " him,

" him, to afk me, with great good-nature,
" what my friends would fay to my love-af-
" fair; and added, ' that, as he could not
" give his daughter any confiderable fortune,
" it muft be an imprudent match for me, and
" that fhe would probably be happier with one
" in her own ftation; and therefore he begged
" I would not trifle with fo young a girl, nor
" perplex her with fruitlefs expectations.'

" I replied, ' that though I was certain I
" could not be happy without her, yet I was
" fenfible, that, as I had only a younger bro-
" ther's fortune, I muft make both myfelf and
" Mifs Woodville unhappy, if we fhould marry
" before I was fettled in any profeffion; that,
" however, as I had a very honourable paffion
" and fincere regard for her, I hoped he would
" not be uneafy at my continuing the prefent
" correfpondence with her, till fomething
" fhould happen in my favour, or that I was
" fettled in fome way of increafing my for-
" tune; and that then I fhould prefer his
" daughter to all the women in the world.'

" As Mr. Woodville was a good-natured,
" eafy man, and I believe had forced himfelf
" to make this remonftrance only in compli-
" ance with his wife, he was foon anfwered;
" and

" and our converfation ended without any per-
" emptory ftipulation as to my future beha-
" viour to Charlotte Woodville. Accord-
" ingly, we took every opportunity of being
" alone together, as ufual ; which fo much in-
" creafed Mrs. Woodville's animofity againft
" us both, that I foon found it would be im-
" poffible for Charlotte to continue long under
" the fame roof with her ftep-mother.

" Befides, though Mifs Woodville had fome-
" thing naturally polite and genteel in her
" manner, yet I thought it would be highly
" neceffary for her to receive fome better in-
" ftruƐtions, in the common accomplifhments
" of the fex, than were to be met with in that
" very retired fituation. After confulting her
" therefore, though I found her delicacy a
" little fhocked at the thoughts of being
" obliged to me for any part of her education ;
" yet, upon fetting the affair in a proper light,
" and reprefenting to her, how unlikely it
" was that her ftep-mother would fuffer her
" father to be at any extraordinary expence,
" with a view to forward a match which fhe
" feemed fo much averfe to, Mifs Woodville
" at laft fubmitted to the neceffity : and, with
" her permiffion, I at firft propofed to her
" father

" father to fend her to a boarding-fchool, at
" a large country town, fome diftance from
" home :: but after reflecting that London was
" the fountain-head' of politenefs, and that
" fhe would be there further removed from the
" fpeculation of her impertinent neighbours,
" I determined (with his approbation) to fend
" her thither. He faid, ' that, for his part,
" he had an entire confidence in my honour-
" able intentions, and fhould not fcruple
" to truft his daughter wholly to my care.
" 'But,' fays he, ' the world will be apt to
" cenfure both your conduct and mine, if I
" fuffer her to go from home before I have had
" fome fecurity for your marrying her. Be-
" fides,' continued he, ' I am certain my wife
" will not confent to her daughter's taking
" fuch an imprudent ftep upon any other con-
" ditions.' In this, however, Mr. Woodville
" was miftaken. It had always been his wife's
" policy, to work her own children as much
" as poffible into her hufband's favour; and,
" in order to that, fhe was continually filling
" his head with comparifons between their
" behaviour and that of his own children,
" which were always injurious to the latter;
" and had a particular pique (as I have ob-
                              " ferved)

" ferved) againſt his daughter Charlotte, as
" her rival in Mr. Woodville's affections.
" She therefore was not at all diſpleaſed with
" the proſpect of getting rid of ſo dangerous
" a competitor, by her engaging in an adven-
" ture of this kind, which ſhe foreſaw would
" probably bring ſome reflections on her pru-
" dence at leaſt, if not entirely ruin her repu-
" tation: for that reaſon therefore, as alſo
" becauſe ſhe found it in vain to oppoſe an
" affair in which ſhe ſaw me now ſo ſeriouſly
" embarked, ſhe on a ſudden altered her be-
" haviour both to me and to her daughter-in-
" law.

" As to my marrying Miſs Woodville im-
" mediately, I told her father, ' that, as I was
" fellow of a college, though we did not ab-
" ſolutely forſwear matrimony (as was a vul-
" gar opinion) when we accepted of a fellow-
" ſhip, yet that a forfeiture of the preferment
" was the penalty annexed; which I muſt ne-
" ceſſarily ſubmit to, as ſoon as my marriage
" became public. As I had therefore ſome
" particularly prudential reaſons for continuing
" at college for ſome time longer, I deſired him
" to diſpenſe with our performing the ceremony;
" and I would give him any ſecurity he ſhould
" require

" require for fulfilling my engagements as foon
" as we arrived in London. As he was of an
" honourable temper himfelf, he was not apt
" to be fufpicious of others; but, however,
" could not be brought to acquiefce in fuch an
" ambiguous declaration.

CHAP. X.

The Story continued.

" ABOUT this time we had an invitation
" from Mr. Woodville's brother, (who
" farmed a little eftate of his own at a few
" miles diftance) to fpend the day with him.
" The houfe he lived in was fituated in the
" midft of woods, in a very folitary part of the
" country. It was a large old manfion-houfe,
" and had a chapel contiguous to it, in which
" fervice was performed once a month. As
" Mrs. Woodville was now upon better terms
" with me and her daughter, fhe gracioufly
" condefcended to accompany us in this little
" expedition. As the road lay through two or
" three villages where we were known, this
" caufed fome fpeculation; and it was gene-
" rally

" rally believed in the neighbourhood, that
" we went thither to be married. And whe-
" ther Mrs. Woodville endeavoured to perfuade
" her hufband that we really were fo, in order
" to facilitate our removal, or whatever elfe
" was the caufe ; foon after this, I found him
" difpofed to confent to his daughter's going
" with me to London.

" Accordingly, after a few days prepara-
" tion, (but without any previous provifion for
" lodgings, or for a place of education to fettle
" my charge in, for I had no friend in town
" to whom I could communicate a fcheme of
" this kind) I fent to a large town, at fome
" diftance from Mr. Woodville's, and took
" places in the ftage-coach, which fet out
" every day from thence to London.

" As poor Charlotte had never been two
" days together from her father before, who
" was exceffively fond of her, and alfo in a
" precarious ftate of health from very frequent
" returns of the gout, the parting between
" them was very affecting ; and I believe there
" was not a fervant, or any one in the family,
" that did not fhed tears at her departure :
" even Mrs. Woodville herfelf behaved with
" a very decent diffimulation."

Mr.

Mr. Rivers was going on with his ſtory, when the ſervant let them know that ſupper was upon the table. Mrs. Rivers had furniſhed out a plain, but elegant, ſupper; and Wild-gooſe, being happy in the company and friendly converſation of an old acquaintance, forgot a little his uſual auſterity, and ſeemed to enjoy himſelf like a man of this world.

After ſupper, however, upon Mr. Rivers's drinking an health to his *friends* in Glocefter-ſhire, Wildgooſe fetching a deep figh, " Ah!" ſays he, " the friendſhip of this world is enmity " with God."—" Well, my good friend," ſays Rivers, " not to diſpute the propriety of " your application, I hope you do not think " natural affection, or the regard which one " feels for one's relations, is ſinful: for my " part, I am ſo far of a different opinion," continued Rivers, " that, however unſociable " I may appear, or however I may renounce " the common friendſhip, or rather imper- " tinence, of the world; yet I think the chief " happineſs of this life was intended by Provi- " dence to ariſe from the exercife of the ſocial " affections. In this our preſent limited ſtate, " indeed, it muſt neceſſarily be confined " within narrow bounds. The pride, malice,
" and.

" and perverfenefs, of too great a part of man-
" kind, arifing from the oppofition of their
" feveral interefts, may make it prudent to re-
" ftrain our connections to a few friends, and
" almoft within one's own family: yet here-
" after our benevolence, and confequently our
" happinefs, will be greatly enlarged: and the
" whole univerfe will probably converfe with
" the fame mutual love and harmony as a
" fingle family."

Wildgoofe was going to reply; when a little
boy, about five years old, with the face of a
cherubim, ran into the room, and, leaping up
into Mrs. Rivers's lap, ran his head into her
bofom, by way of afking *her* bleffing. She
looked down upon him with inexpreffible
fweetnefs, and the air of a Madonna by Ra-
phael or Corregio; and, having fqueezed him
to her breaft, difmiffed him with a thoufand
kiffes. Wildgoofe fmiled; and owned, " that
" was an unanfwerable proof of the happinefs
" arifing from natural affection." And Mrs.
Rivers retiring foon after, Mr. Rivers proceeded with his ftory.

C H A P.

CHAP. XI.

Mr. Rivers continues his Story.

"UPON our setting out, as I told you, Mr.
"   Woodville sent a trusty domestic with
" us, to meet the coach at ——, where we
" lay the first night at an inn which the fa-
" mily always made use of. I committed my
" charge to the care of the mistress of the
" house, who, being a widow woman, let
" Charlotte sleep in her own chamber, and in
" the morning saw her safe in the stage-coach.
" I need not trouble you with the particulars
" of our journey: but suppose us arrived in
" town about the dusk of the evening,
" and set down at the ' Bolt and Tun' in
" Fleet-street. Whoever has seen that ancient
" gloomy hotel (which, however, may have
" been a magnificent palace before the Refor-
" mation) will easily imagine with what horror
" it must strike a young person, who was ne-
" ver before from her father's house in the
" country. We were taken, by a tall mas-
" culine creature in petticoats, into a dark
                                        " back-

" back-parlour, with one window in it; which,
" inftead of green fields and blooming hedge-
" rows, which fhe had been always ufed to, had no
" other profpect but into a dufky court, juft large
" enough to contain an old bottle-rack, which
" faced the window, and bounded our view.

" The moment we came into this apart-
" ment, ' O, Heavens!' cries Mifs Wood-
" ville, ' is this London? Well, Mr. Rivers,
" I am entirely under your protection. O,
" my poor father!' and almoft fainted away
" in my arms. I endeavoured to footh her,
" by affuring her fhe fhould ftay but one night
" in that houfe, and that the next morning I
" would look out for fome agreeable lodging;
" and that fhe would foon have a different opi-
" nion of that grand metropolis.

" We were now interrupted by the entrance
" of a drawer, to know if we called. He fur-
" veyed us both with fome accuracy; and im-
" mediately fent in the chamber-maid, to afk if
" we muft have feparate beds. As foon as I had
" anfwered her in the affirmative, in comes the
" miftrefs of the houfe, and, after viewing
" Mifs Woodville with an affected indifference,
" defired to know what we would have for fup-
" per. In fhort, I now began to reflect, which

5   " I had

" I had hardly suffered myself to do before, in
" what light the dear object of my sincerest
" affection must necessarily appear, and was not
" a little shocked at the reflection. However, I
" again requested the mistress of the house to get
" the young lady a safe bed-chamber, which she
" did in a closet within her own appartment.

   " The next morning, as soon as we had
" breakfasted, I sallied forth in quest of lodg-
" ings.   The most retired part of the town,
" that first occurred to me, was St. Martin's-
" lane, where, upon the pavement, I saw a bill
" up, with a second floor to be lett.   Upon
" my rapping at the door, there came out a
" small middle-aged woman, with a tolerable
" aspect, who, upon my mentioning my busi-
" ness, entered at once into my schemes, and,
" with apparent benevolence, and great volu-
" bility of tongue, told me ' she had lately had
" a clergyman's wife, out of ――――shire, in just
" the same circumstances which I had menti-
" oned, and who loved her as if she had been
" her own mother; that she had two daughters
" of her own, who would be good companions
" for the young lady, and went to a dancing
" school in the neighbourhood, which would
" answer my purpose.'

                              " In

"In ſhort, we ſoon came to terms for
" lodging and boarding; and I brought Miſs
" Woodville thither before dinner, who ap-
" peared much pleaſed with the chearfulneſs
" of the apartment, and I did not doubt but
" ſhe would be here very agreeably ſituated.

CHAP. XII.

The Story continued.

"WELL, I had now this young creature
" entirely in my power; and you
" might imagine, that nothing was wanting to
" compleat my happineſs. But, alas! I was
" conſcious to myſelf, that all was not right;
" and was greatly at a loſs how to proceed.
" There was evidently but one path which I
" could honourably purſue; and that appear-
" ed, upon a ſuperficial view, incompatible
" with prudence. I had no friend in town,
" that I could conſult upon this occaſion;
" nor, indeed, did I care to communicate an
" affair of this kind to any of my acquaintance.

" The next morning, happening to ſtroll
" into the Park, by a great accident, or rather
" by the particular care of Providence, (for
" upon this incident, in a great meaſure, de-

VOL. II.　　　　D　　　　" pended

" pended the future eafe and comfort of my
" life) I met an old friend, whom I had not
" feen for many years. Mr. Hammond
" (which was his name) enquired what
" brought me to town. To which I made him
" fome evafive anfwer. But during our walk,
" as I knew him to be a man of uncommon
" fenfe, a great knowledge of the world, and
" alfo of impenetrable fecrecy, I foon deter-
" mined to make him a confident. I defired
" him therefore to drink tea with me at my
" lodgings that very afternoon; which he
" complied with : and as foon as he came, I
" opened to him my adventure, and prepared
" him for the appearance of Mifs Woodville.

" As he knew I was fellow of a college, and
" had only a younger brother's fortune, and
" that fuch a fcheme muft be in every light
" highly imprudent, he began, with great ear-
" neftnefs, to conjure me by all means to put
" an end to it; begging me to reflect ' what a
" concern it would be to my relations, and
" how probably terminate in my own infelicity.'
" I granted all he fuggefted ; but defired him,
" ' to confider how far the affair had proceeded ;
" that I had brought a young creature from
" her friends and from her father, who either
                                        " believed

" believed that we were really married, or at
" least depended upon my honour to make her
" my wife.'

" Miss Woodville now made her appearance;
" and, I observed, Mr. Hammond seemed
" vastly struck with her person and figure.
" However, he spoke very little; but seemed
" entirely wrapt in thought the whole time
" she was in the room. When she had made
" tea for us, and was again retired, Mr. Ham-
" mond made some short encomiums upon her
" sweet appearance, her easy and unaffected
" behaviour (which was so natural to her);
" then took his leave, and said, ' he would
" call upon me again the next day.'

" When he came, after some little pause,
" ' Mr. Rivers,' says he, ' I have been con-
" sidering your affair with great deliberation;
" and, though I could have wished you had
" not engaged in it at all, yet, as things are
" circumstanced, and as I do not doubt but
" you really intend to marry Miss Woodville,
" I do not see how you can possibly avoid the
" performing your engagements immediately.'

" Though this was what I earnestly wished,
" and was sensible it was what I ought in ho-
" nour to do; yet, I own, the thoughts of re-
" signing my little preferment, and embarking in

D 2   " the

" the wide world with so young a consort, a
" little embarrassed me : yet, now I had so pru-
" dent and faithful a pilot to direct me, I was
" glad not to defer my happiness any longer ;
" and he telling me, 'that he knew a person
" who was curate in a remote part of the city,
" and who would perform the ceremony with
" great secrecy,' we determined, with Miss
" Woodville's leave, to have it done as soon as
" possible.

" Though poor Charlotte had consented,
" under the sanction of her father's approbation,
" to put herself entirely under my protection ;
" yet I could not but observe, by an air of
" dissatisfaction, and several hints that dropped
" from her, that she was very uneasy in her
" present situation. You must suppose, there-
" fore, that in such circumstances she could
" make no objection to my proposal. After
" some decent scruples, then, she consented
" to my request, to complete my felicity the
" very next morning ; which was accordingly
" put in execution. And, it being necessary
" to acquaint the people of the house with the
" alteration of our condition, I ordered a
" handsome dinner, and invited them to a par-
" ticipation : though, by their behaviour af-
                                    " terwards,

" terwards, they affected to believe this no
" more than a sham wedding; at least, they
" treated Mrs. Rivers as if they considered her
" in no very honourable light.

C H A P. XIII.

The Story continued.

" AFTER staying a week in town, com-
" pletely happy in the possession of all
" that was dear to me, I was obliged to leave
" my wife, and go down to Oxford.

" Whether Mr. Hammond considered me
" in the character of a Spanish husband, or
" whatever was his motive, he did not offer
" (nor did I think of asking him) to visit Mrs.
" Rivers in my absence : nor did I acquaint
" her where he lodged, or give her (as I ought
" to have done) any direction where to find
" him, in case of an emergency. Such a
" precaution, however, (as it proved) would
" have been no more than necessary. I had
" often been in London before for some
" months together, and fancied I knew the
" town tolerably well ; but I had no suspicion,

" that

" that about one house in ten, near that part
" of it, was inhabited by people of none, or
" rather of abandoned, principles:

" I had not been ten days in the country,
" before I received a most terrible letter from
" my wife, informing me, ' that she was in
" very bad hands ;' and conjuring me ' to come
" up to town immediately.' I set out, with
" post-horses, the very next morning; and ar-
" rived at her lodgings early in the evening.
" The woman of the house came to the door ;
" and, upon my enquiry for Mrs. Rivers,
" ' Why,' says she, ' your lady is gone to bed
" already. Poor creature !' continued she,
" ' she is very whimsical, and fancies she is not
" well.' As I knew how healthy Charlotte
" had always been, I was greatly alarmed. I
" flew up to her chamber ; and, to my great
" concern, found her in a high fever. Upon
" enquiring into the cause of her illness, I
" found it to be as follows.

" There lodged in the same house a young
" gentleman, of a very sober, modest appear-
" ance, with whom we spent one or two even-
" ings before I went into the country. He
" told me, ' he had commanded a man of war
" in the Mediterranean ;' and I believe, by se-
" veral

" veral circumſtances, that this account of
" himſelf was true. Soon after I was gone
" down, the woman of the houſe came to Mrs.
" Rivers; and, after ſome general inſinua-
" tions, told her, ' that this Oxford ſcholar,
" who had brought her to town, would leave
" her there, and never return any more; that
" it was a common trick among them; and
" that ſhe would adviſe her to make herſelf as
" eaſy as ſhe could.' Mrs. Rivers (you may
" be ſure) was greatly ſtartled; but her youth
" and inexperience was, in this caſe, her con-
" ſolation: for it could not enter into her
" imagination, that there was any one in the
" world ſo baſe, or that what this woman told
" her was true. She proceeded, however, by
" degrees, to aſſure my wife, ' that the young
" Captain was violently in love with her; and,
" if ſhe would conſent to live with him, he
" would keep her a maid and a footman, buy
" her much richer cloaths, and, in ſhort, take
" much better care of her than ever I had
" done:' and a great deal more to the ſame
" purpoſe.

" The Captain himſelf had frequent oppor-
" tunities given him of being in company with
" Mrs. Rivers; but, as he always behaved

D 4. " with

" with great modefty and politenefs, fhe was
" not very uneafy at what the good woman
" had faid to her.

" One evening, however, the Captain came
" in to them, and, pretending fome particular
" occafion of rejoicing, faid, ' he would
" treat them with a bowl of arrack-punch.' At
" this the landlady of the houfe affected to be
" (and probably was) greatly rejoiced, pro-
" mifed how merry they would be, and
" talked with great glee of the approaching
" evening.

" Mrs. Rivers had no fufpicion of any de-
" fign ; but was not much difpofed to be chear-
" ful, as fhe began to have a very bad opinion
" of her company, and of courfe to be impa-
" tient for my return.

" The glafs went merrily round, with my
" landlady, her daughters, and two or three
" neighbours of her own ftamp, whom fhe had
" invited to partake of their jollity. Mrs. Ri-
" vers could hardly be prevailed upon to fwal-
" low one or two half-glaffes : but, whether
" it was owing to her not being ufed to any
" thing ftrong, or whether they had contrived
" to convey any thing intoxicating into her
" glafs, fhe foon found her head begin to grow
                                        " giddy ;

" giddy; so, without taking leave of her com-
" pany, she slipped out of the room, and re-
" tired to her own apartment. Being appre-
" hensive that they might pursue her, she
" locked her door; and observing that the bed
" ran upon castors, she exerted her strength,
" and placed that against it. She had hardly
" taken this precaution, when she heard the
" whole company (like Comus and his Bac-
" chanals) come laughing and shouting, ra-
" ther than singing, up the stairs, and protesting,
" ' that they would pluck her out of bed.'
" She was not undressed; but the timidity of
" her sex, and the particular cause she had to
" be apprehensive in her situation, almost threw
" her into hystericks, especially when she
" heard them thundering at the door, and de-
" claring, ' they would break it open.' But
" her greatest danger was from the abandoned
" part of her own sex; for, when the Captain
" perceived, from the tone of her voice, and
" other circumstances, the excessive fright she
" was in, he very honourably forced them to
" desist from their frolick, as mine hostess af-
" fected afterwards to call it.

" Mrs. Rivers was so much alarmed, that
" she could not close her eyes the whole night;
" which,

" which, together with the pernicious liquor
" they had forced upon her, made her very ill
" all the next day.

" On Sunday, which was the day following,
" she was a little recovered ; and the two girls,
" towards the evening, made her take a walk
" with them into the Park; where she had never
" been but once before, with me and Mr.
" Hammond.

" After walking once round, they came to
" the canal ; and stood some time to observe
" several people who were feeding the ducks
" there. This rural amusement attracted Mrs.
" Rivers's attention, and, by recalling to her
" mind the ease and happiness of her life in
" the country, soothed her melancholy ; and
" she stood fixed in a sort of reverie : but, on
" a sudden looking round, she missed her com-
" panions, and with great terror and surprize
" found herself amongst a crowd of strangers.
" I do not believe she knew so much as the
" name of the street where she lodged, nor
" one step of the way that led towards it.
" She looked wildly round on every side ; and
" her apprehension almost took away her senses :
" but, in the midst of her distress, she saw a
" gentleman come bowing and smiling up to-
                                    " wards

" wards her; and who fhould this be but the
" Captain! His firft appearance (you may
" fuppofe) gave her fome comfort in her di-
" ftrefs: but it immediately occurred to her,
" that this was a premeditated contrivance be-
" tween him and the people of the houfe. The
" captain conducted her towards the Bird-cage
" walk, and began to enquire ferioufly into the
" truth of her ftory, and whether fhe was
" really married to me or not. She told him
" fo many particular circumftances, and with
" an air of fo much fimplicity, that he feemed
" convinced of her fincerity. He then brought
" her towards the gate at Spring-gardens,
" which, to Mrs. Rivers's great terror, they
" found to be fhut: the Captain, however, led
" her through at the Horfe-guards, conducted
" her fafe home, and never tendered her any
" gallantties afterwards.

" Thefe feveral frights and alarms, however,
" worked fo much upon Mrs. Rivers's fenfi-
" bility, that they brought a return of her in-
" difpofition; and fhe, the next day, wrote the
" letter which hurried me to town.

" I found her in a high fever, as I have re-
" lated; but the calmnefs which my return
" brought to her fpirits, and the excellency of

" her

" her conftitution, foon reftored her to her ufual
" health : and, after a little fruitlefs expoftu-
" lation with the good lady of the houfe, we
" immediately fhifted our quarters.

" I had now fixed upon an elegant ledging
" in a neat court, near —— fquare ; which I
" was not the lefs pleafed with, when I found
" the people of the houfe were rigid Diffen-
" ters : for, though the characters and con-
" duct of people have feldom much connexion
" with their religious fyftems ; yet, as moft of
" thofe that diffent from the eftablifhed church
" are fuppofed to do it upon principle, they have
" an additional check upon their behaviour,
" that they may not difcredit the fect to which
" they belong ; and, as their teachers ufually
" take more particular care of them on that
" account, they have generally more appear-
" ance of religion amongft them than the
" common people who call themfelves of the
" eftablifhed church."

" Ah !" (fays Wildgoofe, with a figh) " it
" is of little confequence what church, or
" what fect, we belong to, if we want a true
" vital faith, and are not born again of the
" Spirit."

" Well,

"Well, Sir," continued Mr. Rivers, "I
" ftayed a week with my wife at her new lodg-
" ing; when I was again obliged to go into
" the country: but, though the family fhe
" was now in had a very fober appearance, yet,
" as fhe had had fuch bad luck before, I was
" determined at my return to fix her as a par-
" lour boarder in a genteel fchool, not far
" from the fquare, whither fhe now went every
" day, for the fake of improving herfelf under
" the feveral mafters that attended there: and
" I had alfo given her directions where to apply
" to Mr. Hammond, in cafe of any difagree-
" able contingency.

" I had not been a fortnight in the country,
" before I received a letter (to my no fmall fur-
" prize) that fhe had again been obliged to quit
" her lodgings, after being again greatly
" alarmed, though fhe did not mention the par-
" ticulars. When I came to town, I found,
" to my aftonifhment, the cafe to be as
" follows.

" The miftrefs of the houfe went very regu-
" larly every *Sabbath-day* to the meeting. She
" had not been gone long, the Sunday after I left
" them, when Mrs. Rivers rang the bell for
" the maid, to affift her in altering her drefs.
" After

" After waiting a few minutes, she heard her
" (as she thought) come tripping up the stairs:
" but, to her great amazement, the moment
" she opened the door, in came the master of
" the house. He was a little, middle-aged
" man, of a Jewish complexion, with one leg
" considerably shorter than the other; and
" being of a dirty, though one of the genteeler
" kind of mechanick trades, gave one no bad
" idea of the poetical Vulcan. His wife,
" however, being no Venus, (like that of the
" Lemnian God) he was greatly inclined to
" violate the matrimonial contract.

" He told Mrs. Rivers, then, ' that he had
" a very good hand at lacing stays;' and, seeing
" her without a handkerchief, he offered to
" take great liberties. She was more provoked
" than terrified at this despicable gallant; and,
" bursting from him, ran immediately to the
" sash, and called out to one Mrs. Thomas,
" (a woman of good family, but small fortune)
" who lodged upon the first floor across the
" court, and who, seeing so agreeable a young
" person left in such indifferent hands, had
" contrived to get acquainted with her the day
" after I left her. This spirited proceeding in
" Mrs. Rivers soon put to flight her limping
" lover:

4

" lover: and, upon telling the affair to Mrs.
" Thomas, she assisted her in packing up her
" things, slipped out, and called a coach;
" and conveyed her immediately to the board-
" ing-school which I had fixed upon before I
" went down.

" Upon my expostulating with her gallant
" upon this affair, he said ' that, happening to
" go by the dining-room as Mrs. Rivers was
" dressing, he owned it was a great tempta-
" tion; and, if *God had not given him grace,*
" confessed he might have yielded to the force
" of it; but vowed he had not offered the least
" incivility.' As this wretch was beneath my
" resentment, and I was desirous of causing as
" little speculation as possible, I thought it best
" to pocket the insult, as well as the money,
" which he voluntarily returned, having a little
" unconscionably extorted it, for the ensuing
" week's lodging, though Mrs. Rivers was
" obliged to quit it on account of his ill usage.

" You may be apt to wonder what there
" could be in Mrs. Rivers's person or behaviour,
" that could expose her to so many insults of
" this kind. You may guess (by what you
" now see of her) that she must have been a
" very desirable object, in the bloom of fifteen,
                                        " which

" which received no fmall addition by a very
" chearful though innocent behaviour. But,
" I believe, it was chiefly owing to the light
" fhe muft appear in, as my peculiar fituation
" in life required me to affect a privacy; and
" her prudence and knowledge of my fortune
" would not permit me to keep her a fervant:
" fo that thefe low people, prefuming upon the
" criminal appearance of our connection, made
" thofe attempts, which they would probably
" have been afraid to have done upon a more
" favourable fuppofition.

C H A P. XIV.

The Story continued.

" MRS. Rivers was now fettled in a to-
" lerably agreeable family, where fhe had
" an opportunity of improving herfelf in every
" polite accomplifhment from the beft mafters,
" under whofe care, in a very fhort time, fhe
" made an incredible progrefs. And having
" now equipped herfelf in a more fafhionable
" manner, and being fomewhat improved in
" her carriage (though fhe wanted but little
" addition to her natural gracefulnefs), fhe at-
" tracted great regard wherever fhe made her
" appearance.

" appearance.   If she happened to walk the
" streets, no one passed by her without parti-
" cular notice ; and every young fellow
" thought her an object worth a second view,
" and generally pursued her with his eyes till
" she was out of sight.

" Upon her appearing once or twice in the
" side-boxes, she had several glasses leveled at
" her from different parts of the theatre ; and
" though two or three fashionable ladies of
" quality endeavoured to stare her out of coun-
" tenance, as one *that nobody knew*, yet her
" conscious innocence, and her natural good
" sense, which immediately penetrated through
" the frippery of the millener and the tinsel
" of dress, and saw nothing in those insolent
" fair-ones which gave them any real superi-
" ority over herself, prevented her discovering
" any *mauvaise honte*, or rustic bashfulness.
" And she was distinguished by nothing, but by
" her attention to the interesting scenes on
" the stage, from one that had been all her life-
" time in public places.

" I cannot forbear mentioning an odd kind
" of distress, which was occasioned by her ap-
" pearing once in an improper part of the
" theatre.   She went, with the rest of the
" young

" young ladies, to their dancing-mafter's be-
" nefit, who was very eminent in his way,
" and the chief dancer on the ftage at Drury-
" lane. Having a very full houfe, he was
" obliged to place his fcholars in one of the
" balconies, which, you know, on common
" nights, are generally occupied by kept-mi-
" ftreffes, and people of dubious characters.
" Her ftriking figure immediately drew the
" eyes of all the gentlemen in the pit. Amongft
" the reft, a young man of fortune, one Mr.
" Fitz-Thomas, whofe feat was in her father's
" neighbourhood in the country, and who had
" frequently dined with me at his houfe, im-
" mediately knew her; and, as he had heard
" of her leaving the country with me, and
" was fenfible that thofe fort of elopements
" too frequently ended in the ruin of fuch
" young creatures, it immediately occurred to
" him, that this was the cafe with poor Mifs
" Woodville, efpecially when he faw her in
" that ignominious part of the play-houfe.
" He was a man of uncommon humanity, and
" began to be exceffively concerned, on ac-
" count of the worthy man her father, and
" the reft of the family. However, that he
" might not too rafhly take up with fuch a
" furmife,

" furmife, he refolved to go round and fpeak
" to her ; when he was agreeably undeceived,
" and found, to his great fatisfaction, the true
" caufe of her improper fituation."

" Ah !" (fays Wildgoofe, with a figh) " I
" cannot but think every fituation *improper* in
" that temple of Satan, the play-houfe : but
" pleafe to proceed with your ftory."

" Well," continued Mr. Rivers, " you
" will think I dwell too much upon Mrs.
" Rivers's perfonal charms. But, matrimony
" being ufually confidered as making a pur-
" chafe at the expence of our liberty, nothing
" is more natural than the pride we take in
" finding our choice approved by the fuffrages
" of the world. I will only trouble you with
" one inftance more.

" There was a lady, who had a little daughter
" in the fchool, and who was herfelf a parlour-
" boarder in the abfence of her hufband. She
" and one of the teachers (I know not with
" what view) dreffed themfelves out one day,
" and took Mrs. Rivers to the Chapel-Royal
" at St. James's, where, they affured me, a
" young hero of the higheft rank eyed her
" with his glafs the whole time. And, upon
" their meeting with fome difficulty in getting
" to

" to their chairs, an officer in his regimentals,
" under pretence of extricating them, enquired
" very minutely in what part of the town they
" lodged; in which this lady fancied he had
" some mysterious view: but, as she was a
" woman of intrigue herself, she was apt to
" suspect some deep design in the most indif-
" ferent transactions.

" The character and behaviour of this lady,
" indeed, whose name was Mrs. Birdlime,
" rendered Mrs. Rivers's situation far less
" agreeable than it would have been, and was
" one cause of my removing her sooner than
" perhaps I should otherwise have done. Mrs.
" Birdlime (as I told you) was a parlour-
" boarder; and, as it is usual in that situation
" to find their own wine, &c. and this lady
" was very fond of her bottle, she was teazing
" Mrs. Rivers every evening to join with her
" for a bottle of port, or a bowl of punch; and,
" because she had not politeness enough to trifle
" away her money for what was disgustful to
" her, Mrs. Birdlime had often reproached her
" with her *law birth* and country education.

" I had an opportunity one afternoon of
" drinking tea with this *high-bred* lady; and,
" after being informed that she was an Oxford
" woman,

" woman, and having studied her features with
" some attention, I soon discovered her to be
" our old toast, Sally Burrage, an inn-keeper's
" daughter, who had so long powdered her
" red locks, and prostituted her face to her
" father's customers: and, by a judicious
" mixture of freedom and reserve, had drawn
" in a genteel young fellow with a pretty for-
" tune to marry her, who, partly with a view
" of improving his income, and partly perhaps
" of being more frequently absent from his
" doxy, had purchased a commission in a
" marching regiment, and was now recruiting
" in the north. Mrs. Birdlime, however,
" contrived to console herself, in her occasional
" widowhood, sometimes with a chearful bowl,
" and sometimes, I am afraid, with less inno-
" cent amusements, if one might judge by her
" conversation and appearance. In short,
" though I found Mrs. Rivers had, at present,
" almost an aversion to this woman and her
" way of life; yet, as it is very unsafe for the
" best-disposed young persons to be too familiar
" with vice, I was determined to remove her
" from hence as soon as possible.

" Upon my mentioning this to the governess,
" who was a very genteel woman, though
" elderly

" elderly and very infirm, she expressed great
" concern at the thoughts of parting with her;
" for, she assured me, ' that, since Mrs. Rivers
" had been with her, she had not had the least
" care upon her hands, having found her so
" prudent and faithful, that, young as she was,
" she had left the chief management of her do-
" mestic affairs to her discretion.'

" This account of my wife's oeconomy gave
" me as much pleasure as the vast encomiums
" she bestowed upon her improvement in dan-
" cing, musick, and the other superficial accom-
" plishments; since I had now no reason to
" doubt but she would appear to as much advan-
" tage in the capacity of a mistress of a family,
" as she had hitherto done in every other si-
" tuation.

CHAP. XV.

The Story continued.

" MRS. Rivers had, by this time, been
" near a twelvemonth in town; when
" I received a message one day from a gentle-
" man of distinction, who was then in Lon-
" don, requesting me to bring *Miss Woodville*
" to spend the day with his lady. This was
" one

" one Mr. Wylmot, whose seat in the country
" was not many miles distant from Miss
" Woodville's father's, and who, though much
" older than myself, from some accidental cir-
" cumstances, had honoured me with a parti-
" cular friendship and esteem. Accordingly,
" I took my wife (in the character of Miss
" Woodville) to dine with them at their lodg-
" ings; where she was received with great
" complacency and politeness.

" Upon my being left alone with Mr.
" Wylmot, after complimenting me upon my
" good choice, he, in a very friendly manner,
" enquired ' in what manner I intended to
" settle in the world, if I should marry before
" I was engaged in some profession, as he ap-
" prehended (he said) I should be tempted to
" do.' Upon finding myself thus closely at-
" tacked by a man whom I knew to be my
" friend, and with whom I should have been
" ashamed to trifle; after some hesitation, I
" told him, ' that we had been already mar-
" ried for some time; and, what was more,
" that Mrs. Rivers, I believed, was pregnant.'
" ' Why, then,' (says he, with some quick-
" ness) ' do you not own your marriage, and
" resign your fellowship ?'—I hardly knew what
" reply

" reply to make to this question; but told
" him, however, ' that I intended it very soon,
" as the time allowed by the college was al-
" ready expired.'—' Well,' says he, ' I have
" nothing to do with your conduct in regard to
" the college; but, for God's sake! do not run
" the hazard of exposing yourself to the cen-
" sure of the world, by keeping your marriage
" private any longer. Bring Mrs. Rivers im-
" mediately into the country, and acknowledge
" her publickly as your wife.'—Observing me
" struck silent at this proposal, he very gene-
" rously proceeded: ' I see,' said he, ' you are
" under some difficulty what scheme to pur-
" sue.'—He then told me, ' that he had such a
" particular house at my service, and that he
" would assist me in furnishing it; and that we
" should not only be welcome to live there till
" we could determine upon some better situa-
" tion, but that he should be very happy in
" having us for his neighbours.'

" I was quite oppressed with the generosity of
" Mr. Wylmot's behaviour, not only in offer-
" ing me so elegant an habitation in so polite
" a manner, but also his patronage and coun-
" tenance against the malevolence of the
" world: for he was a man of such a strict re-
                                        " gard

" gard to decency, that no one in the neigh-
" bourhood would prefume to queftion the rec-
" titude of our conduct, when we were under
" his protection.' I therefore gratefully ac-
" cepted of his propofal, told him ' I would
" go to ———, and fettle my affairs, refign
" my fellowfhip, and bring down Mrs. Ri-
" vers as foon as poffible.'—Mr. Wylmot faid,
" ' he fhould go into the country the next day;
" and, when we came, would fend his chariot
" to meet the ftage-coach, and convey us in
" a more *decent* manner to the place of our
" abode.'

" Upon my communicating my intentions
" to Mrs. Rivers, fhe almoft fhed tears of joy
" at the thoughts of returning into the country:
" for, though fhe patiently acquiefced in con-
" tinuing fo long in town, as fhe thought it
" neceffary for her improvement, yet fhe had
" often fighed to herfelf, and fent forth ardent
" wifhes to fee her father, her friends, and
" even her native place again; from which
" fhe had never before been abfent a week
" together.

" As to her father, old Mrs. Woodville
" (you may fuppofe) had foon undeceived him
" with regard to our being married before

Vol. II.   E   " we

" we left the country; and had taken occasion,
" from thence, to aggravate his favourite
" daughter's imprudence, in consenting to go
" off in such a manner with an Oxford scholar.
" Upon my having visited him therefore, after
" I had settled Mrs. Rivers in London, he had
" discovered great anxiety on her account, and,
" with tears in his eyes, desired to know,
" ' when he should have the pleasure of seeing
" his daughter again, and when I intended to
" fulfill my engagements to her.' As I found
" what made him uneasy, I gave him suffici-
" ent proofs of my having done it already; and
" assured him, ' that she was my wife; and
" that he should see her again, as soon as was
" consistent with the end proposed in taking
" her from home.' On his account, therefore,
" Mrs. Rivers was particularly happy in the
" thoughts of returning into that part of the
" country.

" After preparing for our journey, and fur-
" nishing ourselves with several elegant, though
" trifling, articles of furniture, which are apt
" to occur to young housekeepers before things
" of real use or convenience; we set out from
" London, accompanied also by our good
" friend Mr. Hammond, and arrived safe at
" the

" the place where Mr. Wylmot's chariot,
" with two fervants, met us, and conveyed
" us with no fmall ftate to his feat.   As I was
" known to be a friend of Mr. Wylmot's, and
" confidered as a young man, who, though of
" fmall fortune at prefent, had confiderable ex-
" pectations, we were received with as much
" ftaring and fpeculation as if we had been
" people of more confequence.   We ftayed a
" few days in Mr. Wylmot's houfe ; and when
" we were fettled in our elegant little manfion,
" partly out of refpect to him, and partly,
" I fuppofe, out of curiofity, we received the
" compliments of the neighbouring gentry ;
" and for fome time, I believe, were the fub-
" ject of no fmall fpeculation.

C H A P.   XVI.

The Story continued.

" AS every particular of this part of my
"   life is very interefting to me," continued Mr. Rivers, " I may probably have been
" a little tedious in my narration. I will there-
" fore haften to a conclufion.
    " As foon as we were a little fettled in our
E 2   " place

" place of refidence, Mrs. Rivers was impa-
" tient to pay her duty to her father ; whither
" Mr. Wylmot fent a fervant to attend us.
" You can more eafily conceive, than I can
" defcribe, the tendernefs of a meeting be-
" tween a parent, who doated upon his daugh-
" ter, and had fome reafon to fear the event of
" the journey fhe had taken, and a daughter,
" who had never before been abfent from fo
" indulgent a father.

" Though Mrs. Rivers was greatly im-
" proved fince fhe left the country, both in
" her carriage, in her manner, and in the de-
" licacy of her complexion ; yet her travelling
" drefs a little obfcured her appearance the firft
" night. But, the next day, (being Sunday)
" when fhe came down dreffed for church, the
" whole family were ftruck dumb with admi-
" ration. Mrs. Rivers, indeed, wanted no
" ornaments to fet her off ; but a full-drefs
" always became her : and fhe dreffed in fo
" good a tafte, that it greatly heightened her
" natural charms.

" The fame of Mrs. Rivers's beauty and
" appearance foon fpread amongft the neigh-
" bouring villages : and fome of the young
" fwains, of the beft fubftance, who had for-
" merly

" merly looked upon themfelves as Mifs
" Woodville's equals, began now to curfe
" their folly, in fuffering fuch a prize to be
" carried off by a mere ftranger ; nay, fome of
" the moft vain and fanguine began to en-
" quire, ' whether fhe were yet really mar-
" ried ;' boafting, ' that they could yet refcue
" her from the clutches of fuch a mere milk-
" fop,' as, I found, they efteemed me. But
" thefe conceited ruftics had no conception,
" that the improvements in Mrs. Rivers's mind
" would have been a greater obftacle to their
" ambition than thofe in her mere outward
" appearance ; for, befides her having read a
" great deal, and converfed with people above
" their rank, Mr. Hammond, as well as my-
" felf, had taken particular pains to cultivate
" Mrs. Rivers's underftanding : and, by letting
" her into the real characters of the feveral
" perfons into whofe company fhe had been
" introduced, and by giving her a few general
" maxims for her conduct in life, a girl of
" her penetration and natural good fenfe foon
" became furnifhed with a fufficient knowledge
" of the world. And Mrs. Rivers was as
" quick-fighted in difcovering a fool, or a

E 3   " coxcomb,

" coxcomb, as if she had conversed her whole
" life with (what is called) *the best company*.

" We spent a few days with Mrs. Rivers's
" father, in that complete felicity which sin-
" cere friends enjoy after a tedious absence.
" I soon perceived, however, that the plea-
" sure, which Mr. Woodville took in his
" daughter's company, was fatal to Mrs.
" Woodville's peace of mind ; and that she
" had been insinuating to her husband, ' how
" *proud* his daughter was got ; that she almost
" disdained to set her foot to the ground ; and
" that nothing in *their* house seemed good
" enough for so fine a lady.' Though nothing
" could be further from the truth than this
" representation, and though Mrs. Rivers
" behaved with that sweetness and affability
" as to gain almost the adoration of the whole
" family, except her step-mother ; yet I
" thought it best to shorten our visit : and we
" returned to what we at present considered as
" our home, and where for some time we lived
" extremely happy.

" Mr. Wylmot indeed took every opportu-
" nity of shewing us marks of his esteem, and
" endeavoured to make every thing as agree-
" able to us as possible. Mrs. Rivers was in-
" vited

" vited to partake in every party of pleasure ;
" and Mr. Wylmot and I went frequently
" whole mornings a simpling, which botani-
" cal taste was what I alluded to, as the origi-
" nal of our intimacy ; and, in short, Mr.
" and Mrs. Wylmot did every thing with so
" much delicacy and politeness, that we were
" not sensible of any sort of dependance. But
" yet, you may be sure, so precarious a situ-
" ation could not be entirely satisfactory to
" any man, that was not void of all considera-
" tion or foresight.

" I could not bear to reflect upon the light
" we must probably appear in to the neighbour-
" hood (who would not long be ignorant of
" my slender fortune), to the servants, and
" perhaps (though I do not know that it was
" so) to some distant relations of that worthy
" man : for I have observed, that, when a
" man of fortune has no children (which was
" the case with Mr. Wilmot), as soon as ever he
" begins to decline from the meridian of life, he
" is marked out, by his most remote collateral
" kindred, as one that exists merely for their
" emolument ; as a steward, who is to manage
" and improve his fortune for them or their
" offspring ; that he is generally beset by mer-

E 4   " cenary

" cenary people of that kind, to whom he is
" accountable for every act of friendship or ge-
" nerofity ; and that they often contrive to
" fupplant every one, who feems to have the
" leaft fhare in his favour or affection.

" But though Mr. Wylmot was continually
" fhewing us little marks of his kindnefs (as
" has been before mentioned) ; yet it was in
" fuch inftances as were rather convenient to
" us, than very expenfive to himfelf ; and he
" had too high a fenfe of juftice to his relations,
" to fuffer his generofity to ftrangers to be any
" real prejudice to them.

" Another reafon for our living lefs agree-
" ably in this fituation was (what, perhaps,
" you would not have imagined) its not being
" very diftant from Mrs. Rivers's native place :
" for, though I am convinced no woman of
" the nobleft birth or higheft education could
" behave with more true politenefs or propri-
" ety (as was acknowledged by every one
" that vifited us when we firft came into the
" country, and whilft they were pleafed with
" the novelty of the affair) ; yet I foon found
" that the humble ftation of fome part of her
" family, and Mrs. Rivers's former fituation
" amongft them, were uppermoft in the
                                    " thoughts

" thoughts of many trifling people of fashion;
" and that those circumstances were made a
" pretence, at least, for censuring that beha-
" viour in *her*, which would have been ap-
" plauded in any other woman. If she dressed
" genteely, it was called ' giving herself airs.
" which did not become *her* of all people;
" surely a woman of *her* rank had a very good
" excuse for not following the fashions so
" very scrupulously.' If she happened to omit,
" or to be mistaken in, the minutest parti-
" cular of ceremony (which was very seldom
" the case); then, ' what could be expected
" from a person of her education? her beha-
" viour shews what she was; one may always
" distinguish the true gentlewoman in the most
" trifling particular.' In short, as no people
" are so sensible of any little flights or indig-
" nities as those who find themselves sunk, ei-
" ther by misfortunes or their own miscon-
" duct, below the rank which they were born
" to (and for that reason people of the best
" breeding are usually more careful not to
" omit the usual marks of respect to persons
" in that situation); perhaps I was more jealous
" of my little rights in this respect than many
" people would be, and was less happy in my

E 5 " present

BIBLIOTHECA · BODLEIANA

" prefent fituation on that account than I
" fhould otherwife have been. Notwithftanding
" my friend's great goodnefs and generofity
" therefore, I was determined to get into
" fome more independent ftate of life as foon
" as poffible.

CHAP. XVII.

The Story continued.

" YOU will be furprized, perhaps, my
" friend Wildgoofe," (continued Mr.
Rivers) " that, after taking my degrees, and
" refiding fo many years in the univerfity, and
" having had what is called a learned educa-
" tion, I had not purfued one of the learned
" profeffions, Law, Phyfic, or Divinity. But,
" in the firft place, in each of thofe profef-
" fions, as well as in higher life, ' Ambition
" fhould be made of fterner ftuff,' as Shake-
" fpear fays, than what my conftitution con-
" fifted of; and I fancied I had fubftantial ar-
" guments againft each of them : at leaft,
" though I had formerly fome inclination to
" the ftudy of Phyfic, and had made fome
                                      " progrefs.

" progrefs in Botany, Anatomy, and the other
" preparatory fciences ; yet, by marrying fo
" early in life, I had precluded myfelf (as I
" imagined) from a fufficient application ei-
" ther to that profeffion or to the Law ; for
" few people will care to truft, either their
" health to a Phyfician, or their fortune to
" the management of a Lawyer, who is not
" an adept in his profeffion : and, as to the
" Church, the ufual fanctuary of many an idle
" young fellow, the little progrefs I afterwards
" made in Divinity, from a wrong plan of
" ftudy, and an ill-directed application, dif-
" couraged me from engaging in fo folemn a
" profeffion ; for, though I might be qualified
" to *read* a fermon once a week to a country
" congregation, I think it would be much
" better for the community, if more perfons
" in fuch circumftances would defcend to a
" more humble fphere of life, rather than (by
" intruding into a province for which nature,
" or at leaft their education, never intended
" them) to miflead others, by their blunders
" and ignorance, in the difcharge of that fa-
" cred function."

" Ah !" fays Wildgoofe, " it is neither na-
" ture nor education, but grace and the call of

E 6   " the

" the Spirit, that can qualify a man for that
" sacred function."

" Why, that may be true, in some mea-
" sure," says Rivers. " A man should not
" take upon him that office without some in-
" ward call from the Holy Spirit: but the
" most material part of the ministerial call
" now-a-days seems to be the outward call to
" a good living; and, if I had not by this
" match disobliged my good cousin Mr. Gre-
" gory Griskin (whom you have often heard
" me mention), I should probably have inhe-
" rited the advowson of which he is now pos-
" sessed: but, as somebody has taken care to
" misrepresent my wife to him as a very vain
" extravagant woman, he will neither see me,
" nor hear any thing in our favour. I have
" therefore now no prospect of any living;
" and I do not chuse to go into orders, to be
" a curate all my life-time, and work for
" about fifteen-pence a day, or twenty-five
" pounds a year."

CHAP.

CHAP. XVIII.

The Story concluded.

"WELL, Sir," continued Mr. Rivers,
"whilst I was in this uncertainty,
"and undetermined what scheme to purfue, I
"went to fpend a day or two with that Mr.
"Fitz-Thomas whom I mentioned to you
"as living in the neighbourhood. I there met
"another Oxford acquaintance (or rather
"true friend), who had a good eftate in this
"country where we are now fettled. It was
"Mr. Grandifon, whom I believe you remem-
"ber; a near relation to Sir Charles Gran-
"difon (who has fince made fo great a figure
"in the world), and little inferior to him in
"the moft fhining parts of his character.

"Upon talking over my precarious fituation
"with my two friends, Mr. Grandifon faid,
"in a jefting manner, 'that I muft go and
"take his farm,' which was then vacant by
"the death of an old tenant, and was now
"upon my friend's hands. Mr. Grandifon had
"probably no ferious defign in this; but,
"though

" though I was very ignorant of the myftery
" of modern Farming, yet, having been fo much
" converfant in the clafficks, I had conceived
" a romantic notion of Agriculture, with which
" my tafte for Botany alfo had fome connexion.
" I was therefore agreeably ftruck with the
" idea of turning Farmer, and began to think
" ferioufly of Mr. Grandifon's random propofal.
" In fhort, upon talking the affair over with
" him more minutely, I found, that, fup-
" pofing I fhould not make the moft of things,
" it would yet be no difficult matter to raife
" the rent which Mr. Grandifon expected
" from it; and that, with the intereft of my
" fortune, I might live upon it very comfor-
" tably. And, when he found I was really
" inclined to fettle in fuch a retired way, Mr.
" Grandifon feemed pleafed with the thoughts
" of having a tenant, of whom he could upon
" occafion make a difinterefted companion in
" that part of the year which he ufually fpent
" in the country.

" Not to trouble you with any more unin-
" terefting particulars, after confulting with
" Mrs. Rivers and Mr. Wylmot, I came
" down with Mr. Grandifon to view the pre-
" mifes; which appearing every way agreeable,

I   " he

" he gave me a proper fecurity for an uninter-
" rupted poffeffion of my farm, upon paying
" the old rent, which was a very moderate
" one; and we foon after left our elegant modern
" cabinet in ———fhire, for this Gothic dwell-
" ing where you you now find us, and where,
" by the help of an honeft old couple, who live
" in that cottage behind the Elms, and take
" the chief drudgery of managing the farm off
" our hands, we pafs our time in a manner en-
" tirely fuitable to our love of eafe and retire-
" ment. The farm more than furnifhes us
" with all the neceffaries of life; and it is
" incredible, with Mrs. Rivers's œconomy,
" how fmall an income fupplies us plentifully
" with all the elegancies which temperance
" and an unexpenfive tafte requires.

" We are happy in a friendly intercourfe
" with the Rector of our parifh and his lady,
" who are fenfible, worthy people. We are
" fometimes invited by people of higher rank
" in the neighbourhood; but, as I am convin-
" ced, that, as foon as they have fatisfied their
" curiofity, and difplayed their magnificence,
" there is an end of their civility, I give but
" few of them that fatisfaction.

" I converfe

" I converfe as little with the generality of
" my brother Farmers; yet, though many of
" them are people of low cunning, and never
" fpeak a word, even about the weather, with-
" out fome artful defign; yet I now and then
" meet with a great deal of good fenfe among
" them, and a plainnefs and fimplicity which
" is truly valuable wherever it is found.

" But my ftudy affords me fufficient relax-
" ation from the bufinefs of my farm, which
" indeed employs a confiderable part of each
" day, fo that they never hang heavy upon my
" hands; and I really take as much pleafure
" in the neatnefs of my farm, as your grander
" folks do in their woods and lawns.

" Nay, I have reconciled myfelf even to the
" dirtieft part of my bufinefs, and can difcover
" fome fort of beauty in a dunghill; which,
" by reducing the moft worthlefs things in na-
" ture into an ufeful compoft, gives me a plea-
" fure fimilar to that of an artift, who pro-
" duces order out of confufion; or even that
" of a painter, who exhibits a pleafing land-
" fchape from contemptible materials, and
" from the confufed jumble of various colours
" upon his pallet. But I begin to be tedious;
                                    " and

" and will conclude with the poet's trium-
" phant diftich,

" I've gain'd the port, and fafe at anchor ride;
" Farewell, vain hopes!—let others ftem the tide."

Mr. Rivers having now brought his narra-
tive to a conclufion; though Wildgoofe thought
his friend's fituation favourable enough to his
views of making him a profelyte, and was inclined to give a fpiritual turn to the converfation: yet nature now prevailed over grace;
and being exhaufted with attention, as well as
fatigued with his walk, he expreffed his drow-
finefs by a very fignificant extenfion of his
jaws. Rivers, therefore, waited upon his friend
to his apartment; and they retired to reft.

CHAP. XIX.

Wildgoofe queftions Rivers on Religion.

" POX take you! I wifh you were married
" and fettled in the country!" fays the
Duke of Buckingham to a dog that fnapped at
him as he walked the ftreet. This his Grace
confidered as the greateft *curfe* he could wifh to
his greateft enemy. Yet there have been people
who have found happinefs in a country life,
and who have thought even Matrimony a *blef-
ing;*

ing; and poor Rivers was weak enough to rank himself in that number.

Mr. Wildgoofe, being waked pretty early by the finging of the birds and the vivacity of his own imaginations, was impatient to purfue his journey to Briftol, the place of his deftination; and coming down ftairs, he found his friend and Mrs. Rivers with their little family already affembled in the breakfaft-room, into which the fun darted his beams through an eaftern window. The neatnefs of the tea-table, the frefhnefs of Mrs. Rivers's complection, and the chearfulnefs of her countenance, attended by her little Cupids with their rofy cheeks, revived in Wildgoofe for a moment his focial inclinations; and he began to think but meanly of the prefent vagabond profeffion in which he had voluntarily engaged, and could not forbear the tribute of a figh to the abfent Mifs Townfend.

After breakfaft, however, he thought it his duty "to put in a word for God," as his ufual expreffion was; and began to examine his old friend about the ftate of his religion.

"I remember," fays he, "when we were "acquainted at college, you were very pioufly "difpofed; and, though God had not then "awakened

THE SPIRITUAL QUIXOTE. 91

" awakened me, I could not but admire thofe
" who were more religious than myfelf."

" Why, I do not know," replies Rivers,
" that I was any better than my neighbours.
" However, I am indebted to a very good,
" though perhaps an odd man, for what little
" notion I then had of religion : my good
" coufin I mean, Mr. Gregory Grifkin, the
" little fat Staffordfhire clergyman, whom
" you have often heard me mention, and with
" whom I lived for fome time after the death
" of my father.

" My father, though a very learned and
" ftudious man, took but little care of our re-
" ligious education. I had an old aunt, in-
" deed, who lived with us, after the death
" of my mother, that ufed to talk to us
" upon the fubject once a week. But fhe
" generally came out of her clofet on a Sunday
" night in fuch a peevifh humour as gave us no
" very amiable idea of devotion ; for, if we
" did but laugh or talk, fhe would fall into an
" outrageous paffion, and reproach us with
" minding nothing that was good. We ufed
" to read ' the Whole Duty of Man' to her;"
[here Wildgoofe fhook his head with a
contemptuous fmile;] " and I remember her
                                    " often

" often .inculcating to us what some pious
" author says of temperance in eating and
" drinking ; ' that the only end of those natural
" functions is to preserve life ; and that it is
" even unlawful to propose any pleasure in
" them. So that I found the most temperate
" meal I had ever made had been highly sinful ;.
" for I always found that the satisfying
" one's hunger, even with bread and cheese,
" was necessarily attended with pleasure. Hi-
" therto therefore the very mention of religion
" always damped my enjoyment.

" But at my uncle Gregory's I was inured
" to its severities by an agreeable mixture
" of mortification, and indulgence. There the
" flesh and spirit seemed to have entered into
" a very amiable compromise, not to invade
" each other's territories. My cousin Gregory,
" as no man prayed more, so no man eat better.
" He was as hearty at his meals, as at his devo-
" tions. The bell often rang, indeed, three
" times a day, to summon us to prayers, ei-
" ther in the family, or in the church. But
" then we immediately adjourned, either to
" breakfast, to dinner, or to supper ; from
" collects to collations, and from litanies
" and absolutions, to hot rolls in the morning,

" to

" tythe-pigs and fat geese at noon, and to
" rafberries and cream and apple-cuftards at
" night: the very recollection of which,
" at this diftance of time, is no unfavoury con-
" templation.

" The good books, however, with which
" my coufin Gregory fupplied me, being better
" adapted to my tafte and to my capacity, gave
" me the firft notions of practical religion;
" fuch as, ' Bifhop Ken's Manual, the Great
" Importance of a Religious Life, Nelfon's
" Devotions, Burkit,' and the like plain and
" fenfible writers.

" Yet I cannot but confefs, that, after I
" came to the univerfity, by reading the
" writings of Free-thinkers, and converfing
" with diffolute people, I became quite a
" fceptic in religion, and had hardly any fet-
" tled opinions at all : but, upon having re-
" courfe to my Bible, (though I found feveral
" things there, which, from the nature of thofe
" writings, muft neceffarily be obfcure, yet)
" the effential duties of religion are fo ftrongly
" delineated, that, I am convinced, nothing is
" wanting, but an humble mind and an honeft
" heart, to make us underftand our duty; and
" the

" the ordinary affiftance of God's Spirit, to
" enable us to practife it."

Wildgoofe began to controvert his friend's
opinions : but, finding him rather obftinate,
he was unwilling to pufh matters too far at prefent. He began therefore to think of proceeding in his travels, and fetting out for Briftol,
according to his firft intentions.

He had addreffed himfelf once or twice to
Mrs. Rivers. But Mr. Rivers interpofing,
" My good friend," fays he, " my wife fays
" her prayers, and takes care of her family,
" and does all the good in her power amongft
" her poor neighbours : but women, whofe
" affections are employed upon their children,
" and their attention taken up with domeftic
" concerns, have not time for thefe nice fpe-
" culations, in which, I find, you have of late
" been fo deeply engaged, and which feem to
" have taken entire poffeffion of your imagi-
" nation. We will therefore drop the fubject,
" if you pleafe, and take a walk in the garden,
" or try to catch fome fifh for our dinner."
Wildgoofe thanked his old friend ; but faid,
" he could not poffibly accept of his invita-
" tion, as he was determined to get to Briftol
" that evening." He therefore took his leave
" of

of Mrs. Rivers; and, with his fellow-traveller
Tugwell, set out upon his expedition, Mr.
Rivers going with them to direct them into
the great road.

CHAP. XX.

Comforts of Matrimony.

MR. Rivers walked a mile or two with his
old friend, to direct him, as I observed,
into the great road. Wildgoose could not forbear complimenting him upon the apparent
happiness of his situation; and said, " he
" only wanted ' the one thing needful' to com-
" plete his felicity."

Mr. Rivers replied, " that he flattered him-
" self with the notion of being as happy as
" any one can be in this world. I consider
" every man," says he, " before marriage, as
" climbing the hill of life. Every step pre-
" sents him with some new prospect, and flat-
" ters him with the hopes of more complete
" enjoyment. I am now arrived at the sum-
" mit of the hill, and, I believe, in possession
" of all the felicity which this world can
" afford.

" At

" At the fame time, I have a clear and di-
" ftinct view down the whole vale of morta-
" lity; and can perceive, that there is nothing
" very exquifite to be expected from it : but,
" by making the beft of every incident, whe-
" ther fortunate or otherwife, I think a wife
" man may make the journey tolerably eafy
" through this life, and muft wait with pa-
" tience for more perfect happinefs in the
" next."

Wildgoofe made fome objection to the inac-
tivity of fuch a fituation for fo young a man.
To which Rivers anfwered, " that he faw, in-
" deed, fome of his acquaintance rifing into
" Bifhops, Generals, Admirals, Judges, or emi-
" nent Phyficians : but," fays he, " they have
" their reward in the fplendor and the applaufe
" of the world ; I have mine in the eafe and
" tranquillity of my life."

Before they parted, Rivers took the liberty,
in his turn, to expoftulate with his friend on
his prefent romantic undertaking ; and, faid,
" that although he did not doubt his intention
" was good, and that the world ftood in need
" of fome reformation ; yet he could not think
" that any private perfon could be juftified in
" difturbing the peace of fociety, without fome
" divine

3

" divine commiffion for that purpofe." But reafoning with a man under the influence of any paffion is like endeavouring to ftop a wild horfe, who becomes more violent from being purfued. The two friends, however, took leave with mutual good wifhes. Wildgoofe faid, " he fhould pray for Mr. Rivers's con-
" verfion :"—and Rivers, " that it would be
" a great pleafure to him, to hear that Mr.
" Wildgoofe was returned to his difconfolate
" mother."

C H A P. XX.

Arrive at Briftol.

IT was now paft the middle of the day, and the weather extremely hot. Tugwell, therefore, interceded with his mafter, " to ftop and
" refresh themfelves at a fmall inn, a few miles
" fhort of Briftol ;" with which requeft, though impatient to get to his journey's end, Mr. Wildgoofe thought it expedient to comply. He took himfelf a very flight refrefhment ; but defired Jerry, " to call for what he chofe ;" which having done, and taken his pipe according to

custom, Jerry sate down upon a bench, between a Bath postilion and the tapster, and took a comfortable nap. But Wildgoose soon rouzed him from his tranquil state, and again set out with hasty strides for the great commercial city of Bristol; which he considered, however, in no other light than as the Capernaum, the present residence of that great apostle Mr. Whitfield. Here they arrived about six o'clock in the evening.

As soon as they were got through the city-gate into Temple-street, (which gives one no very favourable idea of that opulent city) some boys called after Tugwell, who was a few yards behind his master, "Ha! Jerry! "your humble servant, Master Jerry." Before he could express his surprize, another cries out, "God ha' mercy, Jerry!" A third hollows out, "Jerry for ever!"

As soon as Tugwell could come up to Wildgoose, "Odsbobs," cries he, "why, Master, "our name is up; we may lie abed; I suppose "they have heard of our preaching all over "England by this time; the very boys in the "street seem to know us, and call us by our "names."—"Why," replies Wildgoose, "I "do not suppose it is altogether the fame of

                                    "our

" our preaching that makes us known here; but
" I do not doubt that God will fend his angel
" before us, as he did * before Mr. Whitfield
" in Wales; and where-ever we come, prepare
" people for our reception."

Wildgoofe was going on in his obfervations;
when Jerry now getting before him, he faw his
name, in capital letters, written upon his
back, with chalk; which was a piece of wag-
gery of the tapfter's at their laft ftage, who,
having heard his mafter call him Jerry, while
Tugwell took a nap between him and the poftilion, as was related, had put that joke upon
him. Wildgoofe rubbed out the chalk as well
as he could, to prevent them from being ex-
pofed to unneceffary fpeculation; and they
trudged on towards the heart of the city.

Upon enquiring after a lodging of a fober fort
of a tradefman at his door, they were directed
down to the Quay : where they met with a tolerably decent apartment at a Gingerbread-ba-
ker's, on reafonable terms; though they were
obliged, by a prudent precaution of their landlady, to pay a week's rent on their taking poffeffion of the premifes.

* Vid. Journal.

Wildgoofe.

Wildgoofe, thinking it now too late to wait on Mr. Whitfield that evening, employed it in making proper enquiries after his lodgings, and in giving good advice to the people where he himfelf lodged; and, after eating a flight fupper, retired early to his repofe.

END OF BOOK. VI.

THE

THE
SPIRITUAL QUIXOTE.

BOOK VII.

CHAP. I.

Mr. Wildgoofe's Interview with Mr. Whitfield.

ALL the civilized nations of the world had now —— boiled their tea-kettles; and all the inhabitants of Great-Britain (except thofe of the court-end of the metropolis) were at this inftant recruiting their fpirits with a comfortable breakfaft; when Mr. Wildgoofe, ever attentive to the great object of his peregrination, fummoned his fellow-traveller, Jeremiah Tugwell, from the kitchen chimney-corner, where he had got leave to fmoke his morning pipe. "Come, Jerry," fays Wildgoofe, "up, and be doing; lay afide your "pipe, and follow me."

When

When they were come into the ſtreet, Wild-goofe told Jerry, "that he had found out Mr. "Whitefield's lodgings, which," ſays he, "are "but a ſhort walk from this place.   But," con-tinued he, "that tobacco of thine has a moſt "ungodly ſavour; thy ſmell is as the ſmell of "a tippling-houſe, and will be highly offenſive "to that holy man, who, I am perſuaded, has "been watching and praying for ſome hours, "or, perhaps, has been feeding his *five thou-* "*ſands* with the heavenly manna of his elo-"quence: for my part, I was determined "neither to eat nor drink till I had been ad-"mitted to commune with him; that I might "be the more fit to receive the divine inſtruc-"tions of ſo great a maſter."

As Wildgooſe was thus expoſtulating with his friend, they arrived at Mr. Whitfield's lodgings; and, upon enquiring for him, they were ſhewn up one pair of ſtairs by the maid of the houſe, who tapping at the door, the two pilgrims were immediately admitted to Mr. Whitfield's preſence.

Mr. Whitfield was ſitting in an elbow chair (in an handſome dining room), dreſſed in a purple night-gown and velvet cap; and, inſtead of a Bible or Prayerbook (as Wild-
                                            gooſe

goose expected), he had a good bason of chocolate, and a plate of muffins well-buttered, before him.

Wildgoose made a pause at the door, being
a little dubious whether they had not mistaken
the room; and Tugwell drew back, quite
struck with awe at so episcopal a figure. But
Mr. Whitfield hailed them with a cordial con-
descension: "Come, come in, my dear friends;
" I am always at leisure to receive my Christian
" brethren. I breakfasted early this morning
" with some prisoners in Newgate, upon some
" tea and sea-bisatt; but found my stomach
" a little empty, and was refreshing myself
" with a dish of chocolate.

" Well, my good friends," continued Mr.
Whitfield, " has God made use of the *foolish-
" ness* of my preaching, to convince you of sin,
" and to bring you to a sense of your fallen
" condition? Come, my brethren, sit down;
" and let me know, when you were converted,
" and what symptoms of the New Birth you
" have experienced in your souls."

" Ah! Sir," replied Wildgoose, " we have
" not yet had the happiness of hearing you
" preach; but I hope God has, by some other
" means, vouchsafed to give us some little

F 4   " sense

" fenfe of religion : and we have taken a pretty
" long journey, to learn from your mouth a
" more perfect knowledge of this way."

" Yes, yes," (quoth Tugwell, a little en-
couraged by Mr. Whitfield's condefcenfion)
" his Worfhip is no novice in thefe matters
" himfelf : he can preach like any Bifhop,
" upon occafion, if that were all ; but he is
" come to know how your Reverence will pleafe
" to employ him, and to get a little more of
" your Gofpel lingo, and fuch like."

This difcovery of Wildgoofe's intentions was
by no means agreeable to Mr. Whitfield ; for,
whether he gloried in the number of his followers, and began to tafte the fweets of fuch diftinction, or whether he thought that too
great a number of labourers in the vineyard
might render the foil lefs fruitful to himfelf;
however it was, he did not feem inclined to ad-
mit any more fharers in the labour * ; but
began to complain of the great number of di-
vifions already among them ; " that one was
" of Paul, and another of Apollos ; that brother
" Wefley had preached another Gofpel, entirely
" contrary to his ; in fhort, that, from

_____

* Perceived in myfelf fomething like Envy towards brother H ———.   JOYRN. p. 6.

" that

"that fource, 'ftrife, envy, wrath, revelling,
"back-biting, drunkennefs, and every evil
" work,' began already to prevail amongft
" them *."

" Well, well," (fays Tugwell, before
Wildgoofe could reply) " his Worfhip does
" it only out of love and good-will (as a body
" may fay); we have travelled pretty near an
" hundred miles *a foot* upon this errand;
" though, for that matter, Mafter *Wildgoofe*
" has as good a gelding in his ftable as any
" gentleman in the county; and can afford to
" fpend his own money, if need be, and does
" not do it for the lucre of gain."

When Mr. Whitfield heard the name of
Wildgoofe, he immediately recollected the accounts he had received, by letter, from Bath
and Gloucefter, of this opulent convert; and
immediately found himfelf inclined to receive
more favourably Mr. Wildgoofe's propofals.
He thought he might advantageoufly employ,
in fome remote province, fo creditable a Mif-
fionary, of whofe abilities he had heard no
common encomiums. He now, therefore, began to enquire more particularly into the circumftances of his converfion, and what proofs

* Journal, p. 6.

F 5

he

he could give of a minifterial call and quali-
fications.

"Well, brother Wildgoofe," fays Mr,
Whitfield, " * when and where were you con-
" verted? when did you firft begin to feel the
" motions of God's Spirit? in what year, what
" month, what day, and in what manner, did
" you receive the fecret call of the Spirit to
" undertake the work of the Miniftry? what
" work of grace has God wrought upon your
" foul? and what fymptoms have you felt of
" the New Birth?"

Wildgoofe, not being prepared for a fcrutiny
of this kind, began to ftare, and could not
readily give an anfwer to thefe queftions. After
a little recollection, however, he faid, " that
" feveral circumftances had contributed to
" wean him from the vanities of the world;
" which difpofition was confirmed," he faid,
" by hearing one or two Gofpel-preachers, but
" chiefly by reading feveral good books, and
" particularly his and Mr. Wefley's Journals;
" whence, from obferving the great fuccefs
" God had given to their labours, he found

* This was the ufual form of examination by the Tryers in the
laft Century.

" himfelf

" himself inclined to attempt something in
" the same way."

Here Tugwell could not forbear putting
in his verdict. "Odsbobs!" says he, "I be-
" lieve I understand what the gentleman means
" by the *New Birth*. It is no longer ago than
" last October, we had been grinding apples,
" and making cyder, for Madam Wildgoose,
" your Worship's mother; and all the next
" day I was mortal sick, and troubled with the
" gripes and the belly-ach; and I thought I
" should have *founded away*. Old Madam gave
" me some *Higry-pigry*; and our Dorothy,
" who is the best wife in England, would have
" had me eat some bacon and eggs: but I
" could not bear the smell of victuals; and I
" thought I should have died. But at night,
" as soon as ever your Worship began to
" preach in our chimney-corner, I found
" comfort; and, from that time to this, I have
" never drunk a drop of cyder, nor been at an
" ale-house, till we came this journey, nor at
" any merry-making, nor *sich* like; as your
" Worship very well knows."

Wildgoose endeavoured more than once, by
winks and nods, to give a check to Tugwell's
volubility. But Mr. Whitfield desired to hear

the

the particulars, and endeavoured to give the
most religious turn that he could to his impertinence.   Then addressing himself again to
Mr. Wildgoose:

"Well, Sir," says Mr. Whitfield, "I would
"have you consider before you put your *hand*
"to the *plough*, and *compute the costs*; that is,
"how you can bear the persecutions, the in-
"sults, and mockeries, which you must ex-
"pect to meet with in this arduous undertak-
"ing.   You must submit to the lowest offices
"in this *labour of love*; you must pass through
"*evil report* and *good report*, converse with
"publicans and sinners, and even with har-
"lots, if there be any prospect of their con-
"version.   And I will consider," continues
Mr. Whitfield, "of the properest method of
"employing your talents.   But, I believe, I
"shall send you to preach the Gospel to the
"poor Colliers in Stafford and Shropshire,
"or to the subterraneous inhabitants of the
"lead-mines in the Peak of Derbyshire, who
"are as sheep without a shepherd: though I
"hope my brother Wesley has, by this time,
"been amongst them."

Wildgoose replied, "he should dispose of
"him as he thought proper."   And Tugwell,
who

who (though he fancied himfelf another Timothy, yet) confidered amufement chiefly in his travels, cried out, " Odfbobs ! I fhall like " to travel into Derbyfhire, and fee the won- " ders of the Peak. There is a hole in the " earth without any bottom to it, as they do " fay ; and a paffage into the other world, " which they call, the Devil's a—fe o' Peak.—". " I do not know what they call it," replies Mr. Whitfield ; " but, by all accounts, the " Devil has an extenfive property, and great " power, over the whole world at prefent, " efpecially amongft thofe poor people, whofe " fubterraneous employment cuts them off from " all chance of fpiritual inftruction. But I " hope, by the help of my good brother here, " and other friends, we fhall foon make the " Devil's kingdom fhake to its very centre.

" I am to preach this afternoon," continues Mr. Whitfield, " to the poor Colliers of Kingf- " wood (where, my greateft enemies muft con- " fefs, I have done confiderable fervice) ; and " in the evening to one of our Societies in " Briftol : to both which places I hope you " will accompany me, and behold the wonder- " ful works of God."

2   Wildgoofe

Wildgoose said, " he would with pleasure " attend him ;" but added, " as God had " so far prospered his journey as to bring " him to the sight of Mr. Whitfield, he " would trespass no longer upon his time " at present than to deliver Lady Sher- " wood's compliments, as he had promised " her Ladyship, whom he saw at Bath." Mr. Whitfield replied, " that that was an Elect " Lady, a Star of the first magnitude; and " he did not doubt but she would be an instru- " ment, by the influence which her rank and " fortune gave her, of promoting the great " work which was going to be wrought upon " the earth."

Mr. Wildgoose then took his leave, pro- mising, " to attend him with great punctuality, " both at his afternoon's and evening's en- " gagement."

CHAP.

CHAP. II.

Hears Mr. Whitfield at Kingswood.

AS foon as they were come into the ftreet,
" Odfbodikins !" cries Tugwell, " this is
" a defperate *familler* gentleman.   Methinks
" he and I could be as good company together
" as if we had been acquainted thefe twenty
" years.   But I think he might have offered us
" a bit of his oven-cake, and a drop of his
" buttered-ale, or whatever it was.   But come,
" Mafter, let us go and get fomething to eat ;
" you will never be able to hold out as Mr.
" Whitfield does.   He feems to like a bit of
" the good *cretur* as well as other folks."

" Ah ! Jerry," fays Wildgoofe, " thy
" thoughts run ftill upon thy belly and the
" flefh-pots of Egypt.   However, our Mafter
" does not deny us the ufe, but the abufe, of
" his good creatures.   ' Thou fhalt not muz-
" zle thy ox, or thy afs, that treadeth out
" thy corn.'   Thofe, that labour moft in fpi-
" ritual things, have the beft right to thefe
" carnal

" carnal things; though they do not place
" their happiness in them."

By the time they came to their lodging,
however, their hostess had got a good warm
dinner of homely food; the savoury smell of
which revived Wildgoose's appetite: so that,
the natural man getting the better of the spiritual, he sate down with Tugwell and the family, and ate as heartily as the best of them.

The time was now come when they were to
attend Mr. Whitfield to Kingswood; where,
when they arrived after a sultry walk, they
found about ten thousand people assembled;
the trees and hedges being lined with spectators.
There had been a violent storm of thunder and
lightning; but this was dispelled by a single
ejaculation: and Providence was pleased so visi-
bly to interpose, in causing the weather to clear
up just as he began, that Mr. Whitfield could
not avoid taking notice of it in his discourse
to the people, and to hint, " that the course
" of nature had been altered in favour of his
" harangue." The sun now shone, and all
was hushed; and, notwithstanding the distance
of some part of the audience, they all heard
distinctly; for, indeed, the wind was extremely
favourable.

Whilst

Whilst all was thus in a profound calm for near an hour, every one being attentive to the voice of the preacher, on a sudden the skies again grew black ; and the assembly was alarmed a second time, by a most tremendous volley of thunder and lightning, and a storm of rain.

A remarkable difference now appeared between the Saints and the Sinners. Those whom curiosity, or perhaps some less justifiable motive, had brought thither, scampered away with the utmost precipitation to trees or hedges, or some occasional sheds which had been erected amongst the coal-works, to avoid the impending storm ; whilst those, who either were, or fancied they were, possessed of true faith, scorned to flinch, or to discover the least regard to their bodies, whilst they were thus refreshing their souls with the heavenly dew of Mr. Whitfield's eloquence.

Mr. Whitfield now very dextrously shifted his discourse to the present occasion ; and observed, " that although Providence had, at their first " meeting, so miraculously put a stop to the " rain ; yet he had now, with the same gra- " cious intention, permitted it to rain again, " to try the zeal of his audience, and to dif- " tinguish his sincere votaries from pretenders " and

" and hypocrites : and he did not doubt, but,
" together with the rain, God would fhower
" down upon them * the gracious dew of his
" bleffing,' and refrefh them with his fpirit."
And this compliment many of them thought
a fufficient confolation for their being wet
to the fkin.

The fervice being now ended, though the
ftorm was over, and the fun fhone out ; yer a
good part of the audience were in fuch a dripping condition, that it furnifhed many a pious
foul with a good pretence for taking a cordial ;
and the brandy-bottle and ginger-bread were
plentifully diftributed by the futtlers, that always attended on thefe occafions.

C H A P. III.

Evening's Entertainment.

MR. Wildgoofe and his friend Tugwell had
hardly dried and refrefhed themfelves after their return from Kingfwood, when they
were again fummoned to attend Mr. Whitfield
to the nightly meeting at the Tabernacle;
where he harangued to a lefs numerous, yet
not

not a lefs crowded, audience than that at Kingfwood. He ufually made choice of a different text at each meeting; but, whatever the fubject was, it always ended, like Cato's fpeeches in the fenate-houfe, with, *Delenda eft Carthago*, "*Down with your good works!*" with a denunciation againft felf-righteoufnefs, and a recommendation of Faith alone in its ftead, as if Virtue were *inconfiftent* with the belief of the Gofpel; though (as a great Divine * obferves) " this doctrine of renouncing their own righ- " teoufnefs has been generally found moft agree- " able to thofe who have no righteoufnefs of " their own to renounce."

And now Wildgoofe difcovered the true fecret of making converts. He had often himfelf had the fatisfaction of being followed and applauded for his eloquence; but had reafon to fufpect that he rather entertained his audience, than made them real converts to his opinions. His miftake was, that he began at the wrong end. He went the old-fafhioned way to work, and was for perfuading people to repent of their fins, and reform their lives; to practife the precepts, as well as believe the doctrines, of the Gofpel; which kind of preaching,

* Chillingworth.

though

though inforced in the moſt pathetic manner, was not ſo generally palatable as might be expected:

Mr. Whitfield, on the contrary, ſaid little about Repentance, but laid all the ſtreſs upon Faith alone; ſo that, if a man was, or fancied, or even ſaid, that he was, poſſeſſed of true Faith, he was immediately pronounced a convert, and, whether he *reformed his life or not,* became a Saint upon eaſy terms. By this means chiefly ſuch crowds of Colliers and Chimney-ſweepers were transformed into Angels of light, and became entitled to many a comfortable breakfaſt of buttered-toaſt and tea with the more wealthy devotees, and helped to increaſe the fame and popularity of theſe itinerant Reformers : not to mention the many facetious tales with which Mr. Whitfield amuſed his hearers from Joe Miller, and other authors of facetious memory; and the attractions which were found in their Pſalms and Hymns; which, being chiefly ſet to popular tunes, had the ſame effect in recommending their doctrines, as the like cauſe had formerly eſtabliſhing the fame of the Beggar's Opera.

The meeting being ended, and Mr. Whitfield ſomewhat fatigued, he took his leave of

Mr.

Mr. Wildgoose for that evening, but desired his company to breakfast the next morning; with which Mr. Wildgoose punctually complied. Mr. Whitfield then told him, " he had it " revealed to him by the Spirit, that Mr. Wild- " goose should go towards the North in a few " days, and preach to the Colliers and Lead- " miners in those parts; but that he should " first give the word of exhortation to their " brethren at the several meetings in Bristol, " that he might judge of the foundness of his " doctrine, and give him any necessary instruc- " tions for his future conduct."

Though this was but a proper compliment to so distinguished a convert, and Mr. Whitfield was willing to treat his followers with a little variety; yet, as he found some few sparks of jealousy in his own breast, he was desirous of dismissing Wildgoose as soon as he decently could. Mr. Whitfield, indeed, had the advantage of him in complexion, and the solemnity of his periwig (and a good periwig, as the Barber observed, contributes not a little to the conversion of Sinners); yet Wildgoose excelled Whitfield in an expressive countenance, and a more gentleman-like air; not to mention the weight which an opinion of Wildgoose's

superior

superior fortune would probably give to his eloquence.

Mr. Whitfield therefore propofed, " that " Wildgoofe fhould hold forth that very " evening at one of their meetings;" to which, with a decent reluctance, he confented ; which point being fettled, Wildgoofe took his leave for the reft of the day.

C H A P. IV.

Wildgoofe mounts the Roftrum.   An unexpected Incident.

IN the evening, at the ufual hour, the two Brethren met at the Tabernacle ; and Wild-goofe was conducted to the defk by Mr. Whit-field himfelf, where feveral ladies were already feated (which is a compliment ufually paid to perfons of any fafhion) ; and they feemed parti-cularly pleafed with the genteel, though plain, appearance of this youthful orator.

Mere novelty gives a Preacher no fmall ad-vantage, if there is nothing vily dull or ungra-cious in his manner. Wildgoofe, however, having feveral other recommendations, was

5   heard

heard with particular attention and applause; and his fame soon spread universally amongst the Saints of Bristol; and he preached almost every evening to more crowded audiences than Mr. Whitfield himself.

But his fame was accompanied also with more solid advantages, and introduced him to the acquaintance of two or three wealthy dowagers, and as many handsome wives. Among the rest, he was particularly intimate with Mrs. Cullpepper, the young wife of a wealthy Alderman of the city of Bristol; who, having no children to amuse her, and finding but few of the comforts of Matrimony in the society of an elderly husband, chose to pass two or three evenings in a week at these Religious Assemblies; in which innocent amusement her spouse gladly indulged her. These pious ladies then thought nothing too good for such good and holy men; so that, with chocolate and rolls for breakfast in the morning, biscuits and sack at noon, with turbot, ducks, and marrow-puddings, for dinner, and roasted fowls or partridges for supper at night, Wildgoose passed his time in no unpleasant manner.

After he had been haranguing one evening, with the pretty Mrs. Cullpepper (like the An-

gel

gel ufually painted at the back of St. Matthew)
leering over his fhoulder; when the meeting
was ended, and the crowd began to difperfe,
he handed her out of the defk; and, when
they came to the door of the Tabernacle, they
found a crowd gathered round two genteel fort
of women in travelling dreffes, one of whom,
they faid, was fallen into an hyfteric fit. As
this was no uncommon fymptom of the New
Birth, Wildgoofe approached to adminifter
fome fpiritual comfort, when the lady fhould
come to herfelf again; but, when that happened, how great was his aftonifhment to find,
that the lady in a fwoon was no other than
Mifs Townfend, for whom Wildgoofe had
conceived fo tender a regard when he was acquainted with her at Gloucefter.

Mrs. Sarfenet, it feems, under whofe protection Mifs Townfend had placed herfelf after
her imprudent elopement from her father, had
fome bufinefs at Briftol-fair, which began
about that time; and Mifs Townfend, having
a defire to fee Briftol (and perhaps from fome
more tender motive), had defired to accompany
her in the ftage-coach; and, having been
awaked early in the morning, fatigued with
her journey, and perhaps fomewhat affected at
the

the fight of Mr. Wildgoofe's gallantry to Mrs. Cullpepper, it was more than her delicate conftitution could well fupport.

Wildgoofe, having acknowledged them as his acquaintance, and made a proper apology to Mrs. Cullpepper, begged leave to accompany Mrs. Sarfenet and Mifs Townfend to their inn; where they fpent the evening together, in talking over the ftate of affairs at Gloucefter, the adventures of their journey, and fuch other chit-chat, which, though infipid enough to others, is very interefting to friends who have been any time abfent from each other. In fhort, the evening paffed away very agreeably to Wildgoofe and to Mrs. Sarfenet; and probably, if the truth were known, no lefs fo to the fprightly and amiable Mifs Townfend.

CHAP. V.

Gloucefter Journal.

AS Mrs. Sarfenet and Mifs Townfend ftayed the next day in Briftol, Wildgoofe paffed moft of the time with them. Mrs. Sarfenet informed him, amongft other things, of

" the

" the perfecution which poor Keen, the Bar-
" ber, had undergone from his neighbour at
" the pot-houfe, who, to be revenged on the
" Barber for taking him before the Mayor,
" had gone privately and paid off a year's rent
" which he owed his landlord, and arrefted
" him for the money; by which means the
" poor Barber was reduced to the utmoft di-
" ftrefs." She told him likewife, " that fhe
" herfelf had made fome enemies, by telling
" people, in the way of her bufinefs, fome
" difagreeable truths; but that fhe was happy
" in the flighteft perfecution for the Gofpel's
" fake."

Mifs Townfend alfo, at Wildgoofe's requeft,
related what had paffed at her interview with
her father, who, he foon found, was the fame
curious gentleman whom he had accidentally met at Lord Bathurft's houfe in the wood.
" My father," fays Mifs Townfend, fent for
" me to the Bell-inn; and, upon my knees
" before him, raifed me up, and with great
" tendernefs clafped me in his arms, the invo-
" luntary tears trickling down his cheeks: he
" foon began to chide me, however, as he had
" too much reafon to do, for my unparalleled
" imprudence; but faid, ' he could more ea-
. " fily

" fily have forgiven me, if I had not aggravated
" my crime by taking refuge with my good
" friend here, Mrs. Sarfenet, who, he al-
" ledged, had been guilty of fo many delibe-
" rate affronts to him and Mrs. Townfend
" in her letters.'

" Upon my attempting to juftify this part
" of my conduct (as Mrs. Sarfenet had been
" a friend of my mother's, and as I was afraid
" to return home, where I had been fo ill-
" ufed by Mrs. Townfend); he flew into a
" violent rage, and faid, ' that, under the
" pretence of a great regard for my mother,
" I fhewed a great difregard for him; and that
" it was very faucy and undutiful in me, to take
" upon me to cenfure his conduct, or to be-
" have with difrefpect to a perfon who was
" fo ufeful to him in the management of his
" family; and, in fhort, that he could not
" defire to fee me at home again, till I could
" bring myfelf to behave with more civility
" and complaifance to the widow Townfend;
" but,' fays he, ' I will think of fome method
" of difpofing of you; for you fhall not con-
" tinue with this woman here,' meaning my
" good Mrs. Sarfenet,

G 2   " He

"He then fent the fervant with me to Mrs. Sarfenet's, after taking a very cool leave, and bidding me 'confider of it, and behave better for the future.' The fervant told me, as we went along, 'that he believed his mafter was going into Warwickfhire before he returned home;' fo that, I imagine, my dear father intends to fend me to a very worthy Clergyman's, who married a near relation of ours; which, as things now are, would be a fituation the moft agreeable to my wifhes."

Mifs Townfend then afked Wildgoofe, in her turn, "whether he had heard any thing further of his poor mother, who, fhe was perfuaded, muft be greatly concerned at his abfence; and when he thought of returning into that part of the country?" Wildgoofe replied, "that he was foon to go towards the North, and intended to call upon Mrs. Sarfenet and his friends at Gloucefter; but was afraid it would be too much out of the road to vifit his native place; though in this," he added, "the dictates of the Spirit muft be his guide."

As Mrs. Sarfenet and Mifs Townfend were to return the following day, Wildgoofe took
them

them in the evening to hear Mr. Whitfield; though much againſt Miſs Townſend's inclination, who alſo abſolutely refuſed to go into the deſk (whither ſhe was invited), becauſe ſhe ſaw the ſame Mrs. Cullpepper there, whom we before mentioned as a conſtant attendant of Mr. Wildgooſe, and whom ſhe had ſeen him gallanting out of the deſk the night before at the Tabernacle.

Wildgooſe took his leave of his two friends that evening, who were to return the next morning in the ſtage-coach. Yet, when the morning came, he could not forbear another viſit to their inn, to take a ſecond leave of the amiable Miſs Townſend; which was done with no ſmall degree of tenderneſs on either ſide.

C H A P. VI.

Triumphs of Faith.

AFTER his two friends were gone, Mr. Wildgooſe went to have another conference with Mr. Whitfield, who took him to viſit the priſoners in Newgate, and to ſeveral

G 3 other

other objects of charity; to whom Wildgoose was more liberal than it was prudent for him to be, considering how soon his stock might be exhausted, and how difficult it would be, in his present situation, to recruit it.

Amongst other objects of distress, Wildgoose released from his confinement a journeyman Sugar-baker, who had been thrown into prison by his master out of spite, for being a follower of Mr. Whitfield, and for---a trifling mistake in his accounts.

Another young fellow was confined (as he assured them) only for writing the name of a Country Justice to a petition, out of mere charity to a poor Farmer, who had suffered great losses by fire.

Mr. Wildgoose also bestowed an handsome gratuity upon a poor woman, who had been used to retail Gin about the streets, but who pretended to have lost her trade, and to be reduced to poverty, by so many of her customers having been converted by Mr. Whitfield. This complaint strongly recommended her to Mr. Whitfield's attention, and to Wildgoose's benevolence and liberality.

Mr. Whitfield then conducted Wildgoose (by way of curiosity) to several different people,

who

who were great advocates for the right of Private Judgement, and for the liberty of interpreting Scripture their own way; who looked upon all Creeds and Confeffions of Faith as unjuft impofitions, and as infults upon the Freedom of Human Nature; who were for the Independence, not only of each Congregation on other Churches, but of every Individual on each other.

In order to purfue their plan the better, thefe people had given up all fecular employment, and did nothing but ftudy the Scriptures from morning till night, the precife literal fepfe of which they ftrictly adhered to. There were half a dozen of them, who lived together in one houfe, and had "all things in common" (in which was included a community of wives); fo that they lay *higgledy-piggledy*, juft as it pleafed their fancies: they wore each other's fhirts and fhifts; and it fometimes happened, that the men wore petticoats, and the women wore the breeches; fo ftrictly did they adhere to the letter of the law.

There was one man who had "fold * all "that he had," even his very cloaths (which, indeed, was only a coat and breeches), and.

* Contin. Journal, p. 38.

G 4

had

had " given it to the poor ;" fo that he himfelf was become one of that number ; for he was
quite naked, and forced to fubfift upon the charity of his Chriftian brethren : this, however,
he might eafily do ; for, according to another
precept of the Gofpel, he thought it neceffary
to become as a little child, and, like a new-born
babe, fed upon nothing but milk, or pap
made of the mouldy crufts which were fent him
for that purpofe.   Similar to this was the error
of another poor man, who made it a rule to
" give to every one that afked him ;" fo that,
having given away all his own money in charity,
he now did the fame by all that he could ex-
tort by begging from good Chriftians in more
affluent circumftances.

   Thefe people alfo fhared the benevolence of
Mr. Wildgoofe ; though he and Mr. Whitfield endeavoured to fhew them the abfurdity
of their principles, and the ridiculous confequences which, amongft ignorant people, might
arife from thus realizing the metaphors of the
Oriental languages.   " Thus," fays Wildgoofe,
" the Painter (in Mr. Wefley's Hiftory of the
" Bible) has drawn one man with a long beam
" fticking out of his eye, and endeavouring
" to pull a little ftraw, or mote, out of his
                            " brother's

" brother's eye. And, although we are com-
" manded ' to build up one another in the
" Faith,' it would make but an odd fort of a
" picture, to fee a parcel of Chriftians turned
" Mafons and Carpenters, and piling up one
" another like fo many ftocks and ftones."

Mr. Whitfield faid, " their principles were
" too abfurd to be criticifed. However, as
" God had once opened their eyes to fee part of
" the truth, he did not doubt but he would
" perfect his own work, and bring them at
" laft to the true faith."

Mr. Whitfield then took Wildgoofe into
a very dark ftreet, where the houfes in the upper
ftory almoft met. Out of the middle of this ftreet
they went into a little court, then up a winding ftair-cafe, where Mr. Whitfield knocked
at a chamber-door, which was opened by a
little thin man, who defired them to walk in.
His apartment was fmall, but neat enough,
having a print of the Crucifixion over the chimney. There were no figns or implements of
any art or trade; nor any books but a Quarto
Bible, which lay open on a table under the
window.

" Mr. Wildgoofe," fays Whitfield, " give me
" leave to introduce you to a Religious Curio-

G 5 " fit/;

" fity ; or, rather, if he does not deceive him-
" felf, to a Miracle of Divine Grace! Our
" Brother Slender here is a man, that has not
" committed fin thefe five years."—" Hem !"
(cries Slender, lifting up his eyes, and laying
his hands upon his breaft) " nor ever will again,
" whilft in the body, by the grace of God."—
" What way of life is Mafter Slender in,
" then?" fays Wildgoofe.—" I am a Stay-
" maker by trade," quoth Slender.—" Do
" not you work at your trade, then?" fays
Wildgoofe.—" No, by the grace of God,"
anfwered Slender; " for, though I was bred
" to it, I think it an unlawful calling."—
" Why fo?" fays Wildgoofe.—" Becaufe it
" adminifters to fin, and to the works of the
" flefh," replied Slender.—" I do not fee how
" fo neceffary a part of the female drefs as a
" pair of ftays can contribute to fin," fays
Wildgoofe. " I fhould rather think it had
" a contrary tendency, and might fometimes
" fecure the virtue of the fair fex; at leaft,
" as it does not *directly* adminifter to vice, I
" can by no means think that of a Stay-
" maker an unlawful calling.

" But how does Mafter Slender live, then?"
continues Wildgoofe.—" Upon the charity of
" my

" my friends and the good Providence of God,"
anfwered Slender.—" I am afraid, then," replies Wildgoofe, " your whole tenour of life
" is finful ; as no man has a right to be fup-
" ported, without contributing fomething to
" the public ftock."

" Why, Mr. Wildgoofe," fays Whitfield, " I have fhewn you our Brother
" Slender, rather as a poor foul under the do-
" minion of Satan, than as one whofe fenti-
" ments I entirely approve of. Our friend
" has a good heart, but a weak head ; for
" certainly, 'if we fay that we have no fin, we
" deceive ourfelves.'—" Sir," fays Slender,
" Mr. Wefley has given a different interpreta-
" tion to thofe words, and applied them to man
" only in his unregenerate ftate."— "That may
" be," replies Mr. Whitfield ; " but yet I am
" afraid, my friend, your prefent contempla-
" tive way of life is really not to be defended,
" either by Reafon or Scripture, as it renders
" you entirely ufelefs to the world, and a bur-
" then (though but a *flender* one) to fociety."

As Slender, however, had told them that
he fubfifted upon the charitable contributions
of his friends, Wildgoofe thought proper (to
prevent any fufpicion of oppofing his opinions

G 6.

from

from felfifh motives) to fhew him a fpecimen of his liberality ; fo gave him fomething handfome, and took his leave.

C H A P.   VII.

Theatrical Entertainments.   A new Project for their Regulation.

MR. Wildgoofe, during his ftay at Briftol, faw inftances enough of the infectious nature of Enthufiafm, and what abfurdities people frequently run into who have once forfaken the guidance of Reafon, to have reftored a man of his natural good fenfe to the ufe of his underftanding; but he was fo far intoxicated with zeal, as well as with the applaufe which he gained by his eloquence, that he proceeded with great alacrity and perfeverance.

He held forth again in the evening to a crowded audience ; and, after the meeting was ended, again fupped with Alderman Cullpepper, his fair fpoufe, and fome other company.

The Alderman was a good fort of man, who, by his care and frugality in the earlier part of his life, had amaffed a confiderable fortune.

He

He was much older than his wife; and, having no children (as was obferved), could not find fufficient amufement for her at home: he was not difpleafed, therefore, with her fpending two or three evenings in a week in fo innocent a way; though he himfelf was too fond of the pomp of Cathedral fervice, and of appearing at Church in his Fur-gown, to frequent the Tabernacle of the Methodifts.

There fupped with them that evening a Scotch Officer, one Captain Gordon, who commanded a Frigate of war, which lay at that time in King-road, and was foon to fail and join the fleet in the Weft-Indies. Juft as they were fitting down to fupper, there came in alfo a Welfh Grocer, who had long been fupplied with goods by Mr. Cullpepper; and, having been two or three days at Briftol during the Fair, had gone that evening, for the firft time in his life, to fee a Play. Being afked, "how "he came to return fo foon, and whether he "did not like the Play?" he faid, "It was "fery goot Plaa; they plaad three bouts upon "the fiddles, and the harps, and the pipes; "but there were fome Great Shentlemen came "in, who had fome private bufinefs to talk
"of

" of together, and hur thought it was not
" goot manners to ftay any longer."

The cafe was, poor Taffy (as it has probably
happened to other country gentlemen) had miftaken the Mufic *before* the Play for the Play
itfelf, and fo came away as foon as the Actors
made their firft entry.

This incident, however, introduced a converfation upon that fubject, and gave Mr.
Wildgoofe an opportunity of inveighing with
great vehemence againft Plays and Theatrical
Entertainments. He faid, " the Stage was a
" nurfery of lewdnefs and debauchery, and
" wondered that any Play-houfes were tole-
" rated in a Chriftian country."—"Come,
" come," fays the Alderman, " I will warrant
" you, you have been at a Play before now.
" I cannot think there is any great harm in an
" innocent Play."—" Why, I cannot deny,"
fays Wildgoofe, " that I have been too often
" at thofe entertainments in my youth; but
" then I deny that there is any fuch thing as
" an innocent Play. Every Play, that I have
" ever read, or feen acted, is a reprefentation
" of fome love-intrigue, or of fome bafe and
" villainous action, filled with blafphemous
" rants, prophane imprecations, lewd defcrip-
" tions,

" tions, or obscene and filthy jests. In short,
" I look upon the Play-house to be as much
" the house of the Devil *, as the Church is
" the house of God ; and that it is absolutely
" unlawful for a Christian to frequent it."

" Why," says Captain Gordon, " I am
" afraid there is but too much foundation for
" what the Gentleman says; yet, I imagine,
" his inference from it, ' that all Plays are
" unlawful,' is unjust, and proves too much :
" for, if a mere representation of vicious or
" immoral actions (though with a design to
" expose them, or to deter others from imi-
" tating them) be unlawful, how shall we
" defend the practice of the Sacred Writers
" themselves, both of the Old and New Tes-
" tament, who have recorded many cruel,
" unjust, and some lewd actions, even of God's
" peculiar people?"—" Sir," (says Wildgoose,
with some warmth) " I hope you do not com-
" pare the inspired authors of the Holy Bible
" with our modern scribblers of Tragedy or
" Comedy?"—" No, by no means," replies
the Captain : " I only say, that the Sacred
" Writers relate many *tragical,* and, with re-
" verence be it spoken, some *comical* events ;

* Mr. Law's Christian Perfection.

" but

" but then it is always with a moral or reli-
" gious intention: whereas, I confefs, too
" many of our modern Plays have a very
" immoral and irreligious intention; which
" is a ftrong argument in favour of what I was
" going to propofe, and what I have often
" thought would be a very proper regulation."
—" What is that?" fays Wildgoofe.—
" Why," fays Captain Gordon, " as all Plays
" are already fubject to the infpection of the
" Lord Chamberlain, to prevent any thing
" offenfive to the Government from being
" brought upon the Stage; fo, to prevent
" any thing from being exhibited offenfive to
" Religion or contrary to Good-manners,
" they fhould likewife be infpected by the
" Bifhop of the Diocefe."—" By the Bifhop!"
(cries Mrs. Cullpepper, with fome furprize)—
" By the Bifhop!" (quoth Wildgoofe, with
a fignificant fneer)—" They ought to be entirely
" prohibited and fuppreffed."—" Why," continues the Captain, " to be fure, thofe things
" are at prefent upon an odd footting in this
" country. Players, I believe, are confidered
" by your laws as vagabonds; and, I have
" been told, are excommunicated by fome anti-
" ent Canons of the Church, and yet are per-
" mitted

" mitted to ſtroll about, and corrupt the mo-
" rals, and introduce an habit of diſſipation, in
" almoſt every little borough and market town
" in England."

" Well, well," ſays the benevolent Alderman, " all trades muſt live. I believe, indeed,
" theſe Plays fill the heads of our prentices
" and young girls with wanton fancies ſome-
" times ; but, perhaps, they might ſpend their
" time leſs innocently elſewhere : and young
" people will have amuſements of ſome kind
" or other."——Wildgooſe was going to reply ;
but Captain Gordon was now ſaying gallant
things to Mrs. Cullpepper, and raillying her
taſte in preferring the amuſements of the Tabernacle to that of the Play-houſe and other
more faſhionable places of diſſipation. It muſt
be obſerved, however, that Mrs. Cullpepper
ſeemed more inclined to liſten to Wildgooſe
than to Gordon ; which occaſioned ſome little
jealouſy in the latter (who for ſome time had
been a ſort of *cecisbeo* to Mrs. Cullpepper)
which was attended with conſequences, and
precipitated Wildgooſe's departure from Briſtol.

CHAP.

CHAP. VIII.

A ridiculous Diſtreſs. Advantages of the Sacer-
dotal Habit.

THE next day, in a conference, Mr. Whitfield told Wildgoose, "that he would have
" him be prepared to ſet out for the North ;
" for that he had frequent invitations, by let-
" ter, to viſit the Brethren amongſt the Coal-
" mines in Staffordſhire and Shropſhire :
" though he was in hopes that Mr. Weſley
" would take them in his way from that part
" of England.

" But," continues Whitfield, " to prepare
" you for the perſecutions which you may ex-
" pect to meet with from the Prince of this
" world, I would have you undergo ſome vo-
" luntary trials before you leave this city."
He then told Wildgooſe, he ſhould viſit the
Criminals in the Condemned-hole in Newgate
there, and alſo bear his teſtimony againſt one
or two places where Mr. Whitfield could not
go often without giving offence to weak Brethren ; that is, to a noted Gin-ſhop, which he
                              conſidered

confidered as an emblem of Hell; as alfo againſt an houfe of ill fame, or Bawdy-houfe as it is called, "the Miſtreſs of which," he faid, "had felt fome pangs of the New Birth, "and was not far from the Kingdom of Hea- "ven. And, indeed," continues Mr. Whit- field, "I have more hopes of converting Pub- "licans and Harlots *, or, in modern lan- "guage, Whores and Rogues, than thofe felf- "righteous Chriſtians, who are ufually called "*good fort of people.*"

Wildgoofe was fo zealous to execute any of Mr. Whitfield's commands, and had now fo much confidence in the force of his own rhe- toric, that he would have gone immediately, and have attacked, not only Mrs. Toddy in her Gin-fhop, or Mother Placket in her Bagnio, but even Satan himfelf, if required, in his In- fernal abodes. Whitfield, however, adviſed him to defer it till another day, and to referve himfelf for the evening; becaufe he had heard, that feveral profligate young fellows, drawn by the fame of Wildgoofe's eloquence, were to attend the Tabernacle that night. And "Pro- "vidence," he faid, "often made ufe of the "Curiofity, and even the Malice, of fuch poor

* Vid. Journals.

"creatures

" creatures for their own converſion. And he
" could eaſily imagine, without any ſhock to
" his own vanity, that a *new* Preacher might
" effect what he himſelf had not been able to
" do." Wildgooſe, therefore, took his leave
at preſent, and went to his own lodgings, to
adjuſt his dreſs a little, and to wait for the
time of aſſembling in the evening at the Tabernacle.

When Wildgooſe came home to his lodging,
he was ſtruck with aſtoniſhment, to ſee his friend
Tugwell decked out with an immenſe grizzled
periwig, inſtead of his own ſhock-hair and
jelly-bag cap; and, in the place of his ſhort
jerkin, dreſſed in a long, full-trimmed, old,
black coat. Alderman Cullpepper, it ſeems,
finding how fond his wife was of Wildgooſe's
company, and ſeeing Tugwell frequently about
the houſe, thought there was ſomething more
decent and creditable in the ſecond-hand finery
of a Town Plebeian, than in the ruſtic coarſe-
neſs of a ſimple Clown. He had, therefore,
broken through the habitual reluctance which
he felt to *parting* with any thing, and equipped
Tugwell in that droll manner out of his maga-
zine of old cloaths, of above twenty years
ſtanding.

Wildgooſe

Wildgoose could not forbear smiling at his
friend's paradoxical appearance; but, having
been used of late to allegorize every event, he
was going to make some practical inference
from Tugwell's strange metamorphosis: when
Jerry cut short his master, by pointing out a
monstrous chasm which he had spied in Wildgoose's plush breeches, from which two or three
inches of his shirt hung dangling down in a
most facetious manner.   This was a misfortune
which Wildgoose could not have foreseen; and,
as he had no change of raiment, was greatly
distressed how to remedy.   It could not have
happened at a more critical or unfortunate junc-
ture: as, in half an hour's time, he was to
mount the rostrum. What must be done? There
was no precedent of any thing like this recorded
in the Journals of our modern Apostles.   Wildgoose could not bear the indecency either of sitting without his breeches, or of admitting a
female hand so near his person, in a part so
liable to inflammation.

From this aukward distress, however, he
was quickly relieved by his trusty squire Jeremiah Tugwell; who, amongst the other furniture of his vallet, had had the precaution to
pack up a large stocking-needle, and some
strong

ftrong worfted, with which he generoufly un-
dertook to deliver his Mafter from his per-
plexity, and with great dexterity leveled his
needle at the fchifm in his Mafter's trowfers.

Tugwell, however, could not forbear, during the operation, to make an obvious reflection in favour of the clerical habit and facer-
dotal accoutrements. "Ah! Mafter," (fays
he), "if your Worfhip now had but a gown
"and caffock, or could but put on a furplice,
"like our Parfon, you might have gone to
"the Tabernacle without any breeches at all.
"Adzooks! methinks I almoft long to go to
"our Parifh-church again, to hear the bells
"chime on a Sunday, and fee the Parfon walk
"up to the defk an' it were any Bifhop; and
"then turn over the great Bible with fuch a
"fmack, it does one's heart good to hear
"him."— "Ah! Jerry," fays Wildgoofe,
"thefe are only the outfide ornaments, the
"mere hufks of Religion, and fit only to be
"caft before fwine; that is, merely to amufe the
"fenfes of the vulgar; but afford no real nou-
"rifhment to the foul." Wildgoofe would probably have faid a great deal more upon the fubject,
if, in the midft of his harangue, Tugwell's
needle had not flipt a little too deep, and made
him

him cry out with some vehemence, which put
a stop to their dialogue.

CHAP. IX.

Modern Prophecies.   Effects   of   Wildgoose's
Eloquence.

IT was now time for Mr. Wildgoose to be at
the Tabernacle.   When he came thither,
and was going to begin his sermon ; Mr. Whitfield himself cried out, " Let us *wrestle* in
" prayer for our dear Brother Alderman Pen-
" nywife, who lieth at the point of death.
" He is a Chosen Veffel ; he loveth our Na-
" tion, and has contributed largely towards
" building us a Synagogue."

As soon as Mr. Whitfield's prayer was ended,
a Journeyman Shoemaker, who was a zealous
Christian, and himself an occasional Preacher,
cries out, " Hallelujah ! we have prevailed ;
" God has given us the Alderman's life : it is
" revealed to me, that the fever has left our
" Brother Pennywife, and he liveth." They
then began an Hymn of Thankfgiving, for

the recovery of Alderman Pennywife; but, before they had done, one came in, and told them (to their great difappointment), " that " their Brother Pennywife was *fallen afleep* *."

Wildgoofe now began to harangue with great vehemence; and, as they expected fome young fellows to come and make a riot that evening, Wildgoofe was determined to exert himfelf, and, if poffible, gain their attention.

In order to this, he refolved to imitate Mr. Whitfield's lively manner and facetious fimilitudes.

He took his Text from the Book of Ecclefiaftes, chapter xi.

" Rejoice, O young man, in thy youth,
" and walk in the ways of thy heart,
" and in the fight of thine eyes : but
" know, that for all thefe things God
" will bring thee to judgement.

" As if he had faid, 'Go on, young man,
" and take your fwing ; go to the tavern, and
" call for your bottle, and your pipe, and your
" Welfh-rabbit ; entertain yourfelf with cards
" and dice, or with a play ; then away to Mo-
" ther Douglafs's, and regale yourfelf with a

---

* It is well known how frequently thefe modern Prophets have been miftaken in their predictions.

" miftrefs ;

" miftrefs ; and, in fhort, indulge every ap-
" petite and paffion to the utmoft : but, take
" this along with you, if you do, you will be
" damned.

" ' Damned! for what ?' you will fay.——
" Why, not for whoring, or drinking, or
" gaming ; not for cheating, lying, or
" fwearing : no ; God Almighty is not fo
" captious, as to quarrel with his creatures for
" fuch trifles as thefe : no ; it is for your
" want of *Faith* ; it is your Infidelity, that you
" will be damned for.

" I will tell you a ftory. ' A Roman Ca-
" tholic Gentleman went a Partridge-fhooting
" along with a Proteftant neighbour of his on
" a Faft-day : they were driven, about noon,
" by a thunder-ftorm, to a little public-houfe,
" where they could get nothing to eat but
" fome bacon and eggs. The good Catholic
" had a tender confcience, and would eat no-
" thing but eggs ; the Proteftant, his compa-
" nion, who was one of your *good fort* of peo-
" ple, faid, ' there could be no harm in his
" eating a bit of bacon with his eggs ; that
" bacon could not be called flefh ; that it was
" no more than a red-herring ; it is fifh,
VOL. II.   H   " as

"as one may fay.' So the Catholic took a bit
"of bacon with his eggs.'

"But juft as he had put it in his mouth,
"there came a moft tremendous clap of thun-
"der. Upon which, the poor Catholic flipped
"it down upon his plate again, muttering to
"himfelf, ' What a noife here is about a bit
"of bacon!' He foolifhly fancied now the
"fin was in his eating the bacon. No fuch
"matter. It was his want of Faith. He
"had not a proper Faith in his own fuperfti-
"tious principles.

"I remember, when I was at Oxford, I
"ufed to pray feven times a day, and fafted
"myfelf to a fkeleton. I powdered my wig,
"and went every month to the facrament, with
"the ' Companion to the altar' in my pocket.
"I might as well have had Ovid's Epiftles in
"my pocket. The Devil ftood laughing be-
"hind the church door. The Devil loves
"thefe formalities. I fancied myfelf a good
"Chriftian: and had no conception, that I was
"as dead as a door-nail; that I muft be born
"again to a new life; and that I had no more
"faving Faith than a Jew or a Mahometan."

Thus Wildgoofe went on for fome time, in
the ftyle of Mr. Whitfield: but what was natural

tural in the one, was rather ridiculous in the
other, and had a contrary effect from what
he had apprehended; for there were some youthful fcoffers, who at first were a little riotous,
yet they were foon overpowered by Wildgoofe's
eloquence, when he infenfibly refumed his own
ftile; and for near a quarter of an hour all was
hufhed in filence. But, on a fudden, a little
girl, who did not feem to be above thirteen
years old, cried out from the midft of
the croud, " that fhe was pricked through and
" through by the power of the word*." This
occafioned fome confufion; but the people
about her checked her zeal, and ftopped the
poor girl's outcries; when a young fellow near
the door, who was half fuddled, cried out,
" Damn fuch nonfenfe! thefe fellows ought to
" be whipped at the cart's tail, by G——d! He"
then threw a piece of an apple at the Preacher;
and he and his companions, fetting up
a laugh, rufhed out at the door, hollowing
and finging, " Down with the round-heads!
" damn all preaching and praying, fay I.

" A fig for the Parfon, and a fart for the Clerk;
" Let's put out our candles, and kifs in the dark.
                              " Derry down."

* Journal, p. 36.

H 2   Their

Their rude behaviour, however, rouzed the fury of the Lambs without doors, who began to pelt them with stones and dirt, and soon drove them off the stage.

As the preaching was a little interrupted by this incident, Whitfield took the opportunity to comfort his brother Wildgoose; and observed, " that Satan envied their happiness: but, " courage! my friend; we shall make his " kingdom shake * before we have done with " him, I will warrant you." Wildgoose then continued his discourse; and after he had done, he and Mr. Whitfield were again invited, by Mrs. Cullpepper, to partake of a comfortable supper.

C H A P.   X.

Effusions of Self-importance.   Wildgoose meets with a Repulse.

MR. Whitfield, having some other engagement upon his hands, withdrew soon after supper; and, Mrs. Cullpepper retiring to her closet for an hour, the Alderman and Mr. Wildgoose were left alone, *tête à tête.*

* Journal, p. 50.

Alderman

Alderman Cullpepper, as was observed, by his industry and his frugality, had made a considerable fortune. And though his ideas were very low, and his soul excessively narrow, yet he had some ambition to get the character of a generous man, if he could obtain it without much expence, or any sensible diminution of his finances.

As the Alderman therefore was obliged to keep something of a table; he was glad of that sort of submissive companions, who would express some glee at a parsimonious treat, and, content with a glass of wine now and then, would connive at his keeping the bottle on his right hand, and other stratagems of frugality, which he had learned in his less affluent circumstances.

With the same view, he was always recounting acts of munificence, which he had formerly performed; though, like the Traveller who boasted of the extraordinary leap which he had taken at Rhodes, he chose rather to refer you to witnesses who could attest his generous actions, than repeat them.

The Alderman and Wildgoose being now alone, then, partly to prevent too quick a circulation of the glass, and partly to give Wild-

goose

goose an idea of his consequence, and to convince a person of his *liberality*, who, he imagined, would never put it to the trial; Cullpepper filled up the intervals of each whiff of tobacco with the following ebullitions of vanity and self-importance.

"Why, to be sure, there is not a man in
"the Corporation (though I say it) that has a
"better interest in both the Members than I
"have; though I make no other use of my
"power than to serve my friends. As for Sir
"Harry Plausible, he has a particular personal
"regard for me. (Sir Harry is certainly one
"of the *most agreeable* men in the world.) It
"is not because I have a little interest in the
"Corporation. No, no; it is not for that."—
"I dare say it is not," says Wildgoose.—
"No; I was acquainted with Sir Harry long
"before he had any thoughts of representing
"the city. The Baronet is reckoned a proud
"man, indeed; but, I am sure, I never found
"him so. To be sure, the Senator is a little
"reserved, when he does not like his com-
"pany (and you know, Sir, men that know
"the world are so): but, when I and He are
"alone together, I can talk as freely to him as
"you can to your fellow-traveller here, Mr.
                                        "What

" What-d'ye-call-him."——" Ah !" says Wildgoose, "nothing is more vain than the petty
distinctions which the children of this world
are so fond of. Though we are not all
Members of Parliament, yet all true Christians are *Members* of Christ, and one of
another."——" Why, that is true, to be sure,
Sir, as you observe," says the Alderman.

" But did I never tell you how I got a
Living for our Curate the other day ?"—— " I
cannot say you did," replies Wildgoose.—" I
will tell you how cleverly I managed it. It
was at the last treat Sir Harry gave the Corporation. I sate next to the Member. The
glass went pretty briskly about."——"Ah !"
says Wildgoose, "I do not doubt it. Corporation Treats are the Devil's Festivals."——
" Well," (continued Cullpepper, without
vouchsafing Wildgoose the least degree of attention) " as I was saying, the glass went briskly
about; and we had drunk pretty freely, but
in a moderate way. *Howsomever*, the Senator,
who is a sober man too, began to wax mel-
low. Now, as I have pretty good intelligence, I had heard, that very morning, that
the Living of Ganderbill was become vacant.
So, *says* I to the Senator, ' Yonder is our poor

H 4   " Curate,

" Curate, *says* I, at the bottom of the table.
" He is a very worthy man, *says* I. He has
" been Curate here thefe eighteen years. I
" have a great regard for him. I wifh it were
" in my power to get him fome little addition
" to his income. Indeed, he married a rela-
" tion of mine : it was a diftant relation. But
" the man is a very worthy man.'——' Sir,
" fays the Member, if it ever lies in my power
" to oblige you, you may command me upon
" any occafion.'

" I believe the Senator faid this as words of
" courfe. However, I clinched him imme-
" diately. ' Well, well, Sir, *says* I, remem-
" ber your promife. I have a thing in my
" eye, if it fhould happen to fall : it is in the
" Chancellor's gift ; but a word from you would
" do the bufinefs at once.'

" In fhort, having broken the ice, I faid
" no more at that time. But, the very next
" morning, away *goes* I to the Member's
" houfe, told him how lucky it was, that
" the very thing I had in my eye, was become
" vacant ; and by his intereft got it for my
" friend."

As foon as the Alderman had finifhed this
narration, and received the incenfe of a com-
plaifant

plaifant fpeech from Wildgoofe, he began another, about his lending money to fet up a
young tradefman: neither of which was very
interefting to Mr. Wildgoofe; yet, as his
liberality had quite exhaufted his ftock of cafh;
he thought this a fair opportunity of trying the
force of his hoft's generofity in regard to himfelf.———" Well, Sir, this was very good in
" you, to be fure. I fhall never want to afk
" any favour of that kind. However, Sir,
" your generofity encourages me (as I have
" this opportunity) to beg your affiftance in a
" trifling affair; in which, I know, it will
" give you pleafure to oblige me."—" Ay, ay,
" Mr. Wildgoofe, any thing that is in my way
" to ferve you, I fhall be very glad to do it, if
" it is not any thing very much out of the
" way."—" Why, Sir," fays Wildgoofe,
" fince I have been in Briftol, I have met
" with feveral objects of charity; and, as I
" brought but little money with me from
" home, my ftock is almoft exhaufted."
[Here Cullpepper took his pipe from his mouth.]
" I do not know," continues Wildgoofe,
" that I fhall want any money on my own ac-
" count (for I truft to Providence for my own
" neceffities); but if you could fpare me nine

H 5
" or

" or ten guineas, to affiſt any poor brother in
" diſtreſs"—" Nine or ten guineas!" (ſays
Cullpepper, laying down his pipe) " and how
" can you be ſure of returning it again?"—
" Sir," ſays Wildgooſe, " I hope I ſhall
" have ſome opportunity or other of doing it;
" but, if I ſhould not, as you will lend it in
" the ſupport of ſo good a cauſe, you will be
" ſure of being rewarded an hundred fold at the
" great day of Retribution."

" Mr. Wildgooſe," ſays Cullpepper, " I
" have nothing to ſay againſt the cauſe you are
" engaged in; but I aſſure you, Sir, the Mer-
" chants of Briſtol underſtand buſineſs better
" than to lend their money upon ſo precarious
" a ſecurity. In ſhort, Sir, I muſt take the
" liberty to tell you, that, from what I have
" heard, you are very indiſcreet in the ma-
" nagement of your money, and ſquander it
" away amongſt a pack of idle raſcals, who,
" inſtead of working at their trades, run about
" from one Meeting to another, and take no
" care of their wives and families at home."

Whilſt the Alderman was haranguing in this
lofty ſtrain, and giving Wildgooſe advice, inſtead of lending him money, Mrs. Cullpepper
came into the room, and, finding the cauſe
of

of her husband's displeasure, soon pacified him
with a smile, and assured Wildgoose, with a
nod and a wink, " that any little distress,
" which his charitable disposition might have
" occasioned, would be relieved by their Soci-
" ety; that nobody was more generous than
" Mr. Cullpepper; but that he did not quite
" approve of one or two acts of liberality,
" which he had heard, Mr. Wildgoose had
" performed"— and the like.

Wildgoose said, " it was no great matter;
" he could make very good shift for the pre-
" sent." And it being now near ten o'clock,
the alderman's bed-time, he took his leave for
that night; but at the door met Captain Gordon, who was coming to take a final leave of
the Alderman and his wife, having received an
order to sail the very next morning, for the
West-Indies.

Alderman Cullpepper was so full of this unexpected attack upon his generosity, that he
could not forbear mentioning it to Captain
Gordon; and Mrs. Cullpepper, taking Wildgoose's part more warmly than was prudent,
irritated her husband, and raised the jealousy
of Captain Gordon; which produced an event
which she could not have expected.

H 6   C H A P.

CHAP. XI.

Mr. Wildgoose becomes a great Casuist.

MR. Wildgoose had promised Mr. Whitfield to attend him to Kingswood the
next morning, and to give a word of exhortation to the poor Colliers there.   For which
purpose, he was got up before six o'clock, that
he might give his advice, in imitation of Mr.
Whitfield, to any poor people that came to
consult him.   Tugwell also was ready at the
door, and with his inseparable companions,
his oaken staff in his hand, and his wallet on
his shoulders, stuffed with two or three stale
rolls and cold meat (which the Alderman's
servant had given him), for fear of accidents.
Jerry had also put on his grizzled wig (to look
more solemn) ; but had left his full-trimmed
coat in his bed-chamber, that he might not be
incumbered in his walk.

Just as Wildgoose was coming out of his
chamber, a fat elderly woman, tolerably well
dressed, came to the door, grunting most bit-
terly, and casting up her eyes with now and
                                           then

then a pious ejaculation, and enquired whether Mr. Wildgoose was ftirring. Upon Tugwell's anfwering her in the affirmative, and fhewing her into his room, fhe begged leave to fit down a little; and, after a few more groans and ejaculations, fhe opened her cafe. She faid, "her name was *Placket*; that fhe "kept a little Coffee-houfe, where gentlemen "and ladies fometimes met to drink a difh of "tea together, in a harmlefs way, for what "fhe knew to the contrary; but that fhe had "cenforious neighbours, who had given her "houfe a bad name."—"Why," fays Wildgoofe, "the world is very cenforious, without "doubt: but we fhould take care, not to give "room for any *juft* reflections upon our con- "duct."—"Ah! Sir," fays fhe, "why that is "my bufinefs with you. God forgive me! "I am afraid there may have been fome little "frolicks now and then carried on at my "houfe. When young people get together, "you know, Sir, they will be kiffing and toy- "ing; and one does not always know where "thofe things may end."—"Why, by your "account, Mrs. Placket, you do not keep fo "good an houfe as you fhould do"—"Dear "Sir!" fays fhe, "that is what pricks my "confcience;

"conscience; for, I must confess, I have some-
"times taken money to bring young gentlemen
"and ladies together; and, indeed, always
"keep some young women in my house, to
"assist a friend or so."—"Oh! Mrs. Placket,
"I find then you keep a downright Bawdy-
"house."—"Why, to be sure, Sir," says she,
"that is what ill-natured people call it; and
"I would willingly know, Sir, whether it is a
"lawful employment or not: for you must ob-
"serve, Sir, I keep as good orders in my house
"as any woman in England; and though (I
"thank God!) I have always had good custom,
"and have had twenty couple at a time, taking
"their recreation, in my house, yet (I bless
"God!) I never had any murder, or riot, or
"daggers-drawing, since I have been in busi-
"ness. Then I make my poor Lambs read
"the Bible every Sunday, and go to church
"in their turn; and, in short, though their
"bodies may be polluted, I take great care of
"their souls: and I hope God will wink at
"my poor Lambs that *sport themselves toge-*
"*ther.*"—"Why," says Wildgoose, "without
"doubt, our outward actions are indifferent in
"themselves; and it is the heart that God
"chiefly regards. God *sees* no sin in the *Elect.*
"If

" If we have true Faith, that will sanctify our
" works. Thus Rahab the harlot, you know,
" was accepted through Faith. But, as yours
" is an uncommon case, I will consult Mr.
" Whitfield upon it."—" Ah! God help me!"
says Mrs. Placket; " I am afraid I am not
" long for this world; and what will become
" of my poor Lambs, when I am gone to my
" dear Redeemer?"

Whilst Wildgoose was engaged in this conference, in comes the poor girl that was pricked
through and through, by the power of the
Word, at his last preachment, attended by her
mother. The girl looked very pale, and, upon
coming before Wildgoose, was taken with an
hysteric fit. Wildgoose bid the mother, " not
" be frightened; for, as Mr. Whitfield had af-
" sured him, these were common symptoms of
" the New Birth."—" Lack-a-day! Sir," says
the mother, " I wish it may be nothing more
" than the New Birth. But I have been very
" much terrified; and am sadly afraid my poor
" girl is with child."—" With child!" says
Wildgoose; " why, she is a mere child herself."
" Ah! Sir," says the mother, " so she is in-
" deed; for though she is a fine-grown girl,
" yet, if she lives to Lammas-day next, she
" will

" will be but fourteen years old, as sure as eggs
" is eggs. But a wicked rogue of a Sailor,
" who promised her marriage, I am afraid, has
" had *cardinal knowledge* of her, and has now
" left her; and I shall never be able to main-
" tain her and her child: times are so hard,
" and money so scarce, I can hardly maintain
" myself."——The case was, the poor woman
had heard of Wildgoose's generosity, and was
in hopes of partaking of his bounty, and therefore brought her daughter under pretence of
consulting him as a Casuist. But he, having at
present neither silver nor gold, gave her only
some spiritual comfort; and told her, " that
" this accident was probably a very providen-
" tial thing for her daughter, as it was a
" maxim with Mr. Whitfield, ' The greater
" the Sinner, the greater the Saint;' that she
" had nothing to do but to lay *hold* on Christ,
" as Mary Magdalen did, by an active Faith;
" and she would enter into the Kingdom of
" Heaven, before those self-righteous, good sort
" of women, who fancy they need no re-
" pentance."

These customers were hardly retired, when
a dirty-looking fellow was introduced by Tugwell, who, peeping round the room and shut-
ting

ting the door, spoke in a low voice to Wildgoose, and said, " his was a scruple of a par-
" ticular kind, upon which a friend had de-
" sired him to consult Mr. Wildgoose."—
" Well, what is it ?" says Wildgoose.—" Why,
" Sir, whether it is not fighting against God,
" for a man in gaol to use means for making his
" escape *."—Wildgoose, after a short pause,
answered, " that, doubtless, self-preservation
" was the first law of Nature; and a man
" prison, it should seem, might use all lawful
" means to gain his liberty; but Nature is
" one thing, and Grace another. A good
" Christian must submit to every ordinance
" of man, as the dispensation of Providence;
" and if he is committed to prison by legal
" authority, I question whether any other
" authority can innocently set him free. But,
" as this is a dubious point, Mr. Whitfield
" and I will determine it by lot."—" Ah !" says
the fellow, " it is too late to cast lots about
" the matter; for I made my escape from Sa-
" lisbury gaol last spring, and am now going
" on ship-board, but should be glad to go
" with a quiet conscience."

* Vid. Journal, p. 99.

Before

Before this man had done, a tall lanthern-jawed fellow, whose features seemed lenghtened by a long weather-beaten wig, which hung below his cheek-bones, desired to lay his case before Mr. Wildgoose, when the other was dismissed. He said, " he was bred a Dissenter, " and a Button-maker by trade; and in his ap-" prenticeship had married an elderly woman, " with a little money; but she was so bad-" tempered a woman," (continued he) " that " I could not possibly live with her: so I went " and worked in London, where, upon hear-" ing Mr. Wesley, I became a new man; " and, meeting with a very *sober* young woman " of my own trade at the Tabernacle, to whom " I honestly told my situation, we agreed to " live together for some years, and have had " several children: but she is lately dead; and " now my conscience pricks me, and I cannot " be easy day nor night: but still, I hope, Sir, " *God will sanctify every dispensation **."

" What became of the old woman, then?" says Mr. Wildgoose.—" Why, Sir," says he, " as I had got me another wife, I believe she " got herself another husband, more agreeable " to her own age."—" And so," says Wild-

* A real Fact.

goose,

goofe, " by putting away your wife without
" a fufficient caufe, you have caufed her to
" commit adultery."—Why," fays the Button-
maker, " I am afraid I have; but I hope *God*
" *will fanctify every difpenfation.*"—" Friend,"
replies Wildgoofe, " God cannot fanctify
" adultery. You muft confefs yourfelf a vile
" finner, and *lay hold* on Chrift by Faith; for
" you can have no hopes but in him, who
" came into the world to fave finners."

CHAP. XII.

Some unexpected Incidents.

WILDGOOSE, though not difpleafed with
observing the good he was likely to do
by awakening fo many wicked finners, was
almoft tired of his company; when in came
Mrs. Cullpepper's maid, curtfeying and fim-
pering, with her Lady's compliments: and, before Wildgoofe could afk how fhe did, produced
a little packet, carefully fealed up; which
being opened, to his furprize he found it con-
tained five guineas, with the following billet:

" My

"My dear Brother,

"Give me leave to contribute my mite to-
"wards the great work which is going to be
"wrought upon the earth; but do not come
"any more to our house, till you hear further
"from your sister in the Lord,

"RACHAEL CULLPEPPER."

Wildgoose could not recollect any precedent
in Mr. Wesley's or Mr. Whitfield's Journals
of their having received money for their private
occasions: as he was conscious, however, that
his intentions were charitable, he did not re-
fuse so seasonable a supply. He therefore returned his compliments to Mrs. Cullpepper,
with thanks for the contents of her packet; but
was less pleased with the present which he had
received, than shocked with the hint that accompanied it, not to repeat his visits to Mrs. Cullpepper.

Wildgoose was now come out into the pas-
sage, and was observing to Tugwell, "that
"the Spirit testified he should do great things
"in Bristol; and that he had a Call to tarry
"in that city many days." To which Tugwell seemed to have no manner of objection.

But, while they were yet speaking, another
ill-looking Irish Sailor, with one eye, and several

veral fcars on his cheek, came to confult Wildgoofe. He faid, " he had been the vileft of
" finners" (to which confeffion his appearance
bore fufficient teftimony); " that he had been
" guilty of every kind of uncleannefs; nay,
" that, when on fhip-board, he had an intrigue
" with a cat."—" Aye," fays Tugwell, " and
" fhe has left fome tokens of her kindnefs upon
" thy cheeks."—" But," fays the Sailor, " not-
" withftanding my fins are fo numerous, I am
" fo far from any forrow, or contrition, that my
" greateft affliction is the being violently ad-
" dicted to *laughing*, which, I am afraid, is
" a token of Reprobation. Now, I fhould
" be glad to know, whether Laughing be any
" fin or not; for I have heard, that Adam
" never *laughed* before the Fall."

Wildgoofe ftared with aftonifhment at this
ftrange Penitent : but Tugwell, who was impatient to get to breakfaft, ufed this gentleman
with lefs politenefs. " Come, come, friend,"
fays he, " this is no time for *laughing*; we
" have more ferious matters upon our hands;
" you had better be going about your bufinefs."
He then thruft him towards the door. Upon
which the Sailor gave the fignal with a Boat-
fwain's whiftle, and in rufhed four or five ftout
fellows,

fellows, amongſt whom was the man that had
eſcaped from Saliſbury gaol. He immediately
thruſt an handkerchief into Tugwell's mouth;
pulled his long wig over his eyes; twiſted the
wallet, which hung over his ſhoulder, round his
neck; and muffled him up in ſuch a manner,
that he could not make any ſort of reſiſtance.
Some of the reſt ſecured Wildgooſe, who never
offered to interrupt them; and led them both
to a covered boat, which lay ready on the Quay,
and rowed away immediately for Kingroad;
where when they arrived, they put the two
Pilgrims aboard a large ſhip, which was riding
at anchor, and which ſet ſail the moment they
were on board.

CHAP. XIII.

Event of their Voyage.

WILDGOOSE was ſo well prepared to
ſubmit to the various diſpenſations of
Providence, that he appeared quite calm upon
the occaſion, and let the Sailors diſpoſe of him
as they pleaſed. But Tugwell, being leſs paſ-
ſive, ſtruggled, and hung an a—ſe, and laid

S   about

about him as well as he could; for which re-
fractory behaviour, he got three or four hearty
knocks on the pate: but, as soon as he was re-
stored to the use of his tongue, he expressed the
transports of his grief and rage in a most vociferous manner. Sometimes he lamented the
forlorn condition of his poor wife Dorothy;
then fell foul upon Mr. Wildgoose, for seducing
him from home; then cursed himself, for leaving his Cobler's stall, and his own chimney-
corner, to go rambling about the country: in
short, though Jerry had read books of travels
with so much pleasure, and often wished to
accompany the adventurer in his voyages as he
perused them in his own stall; yet he found, in
fact, the company of Sailors, upon this occasion, not so agreeable as he expected.

Wildgoose endeavoured to comfort his fel-
low-sufferer, and desired him, " to trust to Pro-
" vidence, who would bring them," he said,
" to the haven where they *should* be." And,
notwithstanding Wildgoose so lately felt a Call
to remain in Bristol; yet he was now convinced, that he was chosen for some more important service, and was to " preach the Gos-
" pel in other *cities also* *."

* Journals.

Whilst

Whilst they were thus engaged in lamentations on one side, and consolations on the other, the ship was falling gently down the channel; when who should come into the cabin, where the two Pilgrims were stowed, but their old acquaintance Captain Gordon? The Captain started back; and, affecting some little surprize, "Ha!" cries he, "what, Mr. Wildgoose! "what, was it for this, then, that our friend "Cullpepper sent my rascals a guinea to drink "this morning? I was surprized at his gene- "rosity. Well, Sir, he has played you a co- "mical trick; for I am going a pretty long "voyage."——Wildgoose, after expressing his surprize, answered, "that he did not know how "he had offended the Alderman: but, how- "ever," continues he, "I am convinced, that "Providence has some important end to serve "by this dispensation, to whatever part of the "world I shall be transported."——"Why, Sir," says the Captain, "I am bound for North- "America, and am to join the fleet in the "gulph of St. Lawrence. But, as I am to "touch at Corke or Kinsale, to lay in more "provisions, if you chuse it, I can set you on "shore in that part of Ireland."——Wildgoose thanked the Captain for his civility, not suspecting

pecting that this had been a scheme concerted between him and the Alderman; the Captain being jealous of him, as a rival in Mrs. Cullpepper's good graces; and the Alderman being suspicious, that his wife might supply him with *that* money which *he* had refused him.

When Tugwell heard of being set on shore in Ireland, he renewed his lamentations, and made sure of having his throat cut by *Papishes* and wild Irish: " and, if they should be carried " into America, he did not doubt," he said, " but they should be left upon some desolate " island, as Robinson Crusoe was, amongst " the wild Indians; and perhaps be roasted " alive, and have their bones picked by " *Hannibals* and *Scavengers*" (so Jerry called the Cannibals and Savages), " as he feared his " poor son Joseph was." The Captain bid him, " not be afraid, for that they should not " be used ill in any respect." He advised them therefore " to come out of their cabin, and " take a walk upon deck;" where, the weather being fine, the water calm, and the vessel now in the midst of the Channel, between the two opposite coasts, they had no unpleasant voyage for some hours.

Towards the evening, being got near the mouth of the Channel, the afternoon having been exceffively hot, fome black clouds began to rife towards the South-Eaft, and a moft violent thunder-ftorm foon after enfued, which lafted for feveral hours. Thofe who delight in defcriptions of this kind may have recourfe to any of the Epic Poets, ancient or modern. I fhall only obferve, that, after being driven from their courfe, and toffed about a good part of the night, they found themfelves, at break of day, near the Glamorganfhire coaft; and found it convenient (as their tackling had fuffered a little) to come to an anchor in the Bay of Cardiff, where the Captain, having carried the jeft far enough, gave Wildgoofe and his friend leave to be fet on fhore; which favour, when he heard they were on the coaft of Wales, Wildgoofe gladly accepted of. After giving them the word of exhortation, therefore, Wildgoofe took his leave of Captain Gordon, thanked him for bringing them to the haven where he wifhed to be; and he and his fellow-traveller were fafely fet on fhore.

END OF BOOK VII.

THE

THE
SPIRITUAL QUIXOTE.

BOOK VIII.

CHAP. I.

The two Pilgrims arrive at Cardiff.

MR. Wildgoofe now thought himfelf a
fecond St. Paul; and that, in the
late ftorm, God had given the lives of
all thofe that failed with him to the force of his
prayers; though every common Sailor knew
there had been no real danger.

As for Tugwell, he was fo fick at the coming on of the ftorm, that he had not been very
attentive to what had paffed; and was fo rejoiced
at reaching land again, that he dropped all
refentment againft the authors of this calamity.
He had thrown off his great wig; but, grafping
his oaken ftaff, and fecuring his wallet, he
fprang eagerly upon the fhore, without looking

behind

behind him; and, defirous as he had formerly
been of travelling, made a folemn vow, "never
"to forfake the *terra firma* again as long as he
"lived."

The place where they landed was about
three-miles from Cardiff; and, it being early
in the morning, and no living creature to be
feen, Tugwell began again to wifh himfelf
at home, in his own chimney-corner, with a
mefs of onion-pottage, or a difh of Madam
Wildgoofe's pot-liquor, for his breakfaft; for,
having eaten nothing the whole preceding day
but a fea-bifcuit, he began to complain of hunger and fatigue. By good luck, however, upon
fearching his wallet, he found a couple of rolls
and a piece of mutton-pye, which he had laid
in at Briftol: he prevailed upon his mafter,
therefore, without much difficulty, to fit down
at the foot of a rock, and partake with him of
what he had fo providently laid in.

But, during their fhort repaft, Wildgoofe
began to blame himfelf, for having lived too lux-
urioufly at Briftol; obferving, "that regular
"dinners and hot fuppers were by no means
"expedient for thofe that were called to preach
"the Gofpel."—"Odzooks!" cries Tugwell;
"why, I did not fee but Mr. Whitfield, and
"other

" other good Chriftians, eat and drank as well
" as we; and much good may it do them ! I
" would have every one have a belly-full. To
" be fure, Madam Cullpepper keeps a good
" houfe, and gave me many a good meal, and
" money befides, for that matter."

Wildgoofe, upon hearing that Mrs. Cullpepper's generofity had extended to his companion alfo, condemned himfelf for difcovering
his neceffity to the Alderman; and began to
fufpect, that fome jealoufy of this kind (for
he had no idea of any other) might be the
caufe of his getting them kidnapped, and fent
on fhip-board. He comforted himfelf, however,
with the uprightnefs of his intentions, and with
the conviction that the money would be fpent
in a good caufe; and that he fhould make a
better ufe of the unrighteous Mammon than
thofe to whom it properly belonged.

Though the fun was rifen above the horizon,
it was not yet four o'clock; and the two Pilgrims having had little reft in the night, Wildgoofe leaned againft the rock, and took a fhort
nap; and Tugwell, being now at eafe, laid
himfelf down on his wallet, and, according to
cuftom, fnored moft profoundly.

Wildgoofe

Wildgoose, however, having paid a flight compliment to nature, and having in his fleep dreamed of nothing but fpiritual conquefts, ftarts up, and roufes his fellow traveller. "Come, Jerry," cries he, " this is no time " for fleep ; up, and be doing: the whole land " of Canaan lies before us; we muft fubdue " the idolatrous nations, the Hivites, the Pe-" rizzites, and the Jebufites. God has called " us into Wales ; and I make no doubt that " he will fend his angel before us (as he did " before Mr. Whitfield *); and we fhall " go on from city to city (like Jofhua) ; and the " Devil's ftrong holds will fall down at our " preaching, as the walls of Jericho did at the " found of the Rams-horns †."

Notwithftanding this fpiritual rant, Tugwell grumbled at being waked fo foon, and faid, " he did not find that conquering cities " was fo eafy a matter. You know, Mafter," fays he, " you talked of conquering the city " of Briftol ; but, I think, they have *conquered* " us, and have tranfported us into this hea-" thenifh country, without our own confent, " where there is nothing to be got, as I can " fee, for love or money."

The

The truth was, Jerry liked travelling well enough in a country where they could meet with refreshment at every ale-house; but, having been very sick in his voyage, and being a little chagrined at the desolate appearance of the sea-coast, compared with the pleasures of Alderman Cullpepper's kitchen, he could not forbear venting his spleen against Wildgoose, for seducing him so far from home.

But the same cause, which damped Tugwell's spirits, roused Wildgoose's zeal. He languished for a little persecution (as Mr. Whitfield had often done); and thought things were not right, whilst they went on so smoothly at Bristol. He said, " the primitive Saints were made " perfect by sufferings; and, I dare say, Jerry, " you yourself will be the better for this slight " persecution for the Gospel's sake."—" Yes, " to be sure," says Tugwell; " I suppose, " Master, you would be glad to see me ducked " in an horse-pond, or tossed in a blanket, for " the Gospel's sake: but I do not see what " occasion I have to run my head against a " wall, when I can get my living very well " by mending shoes; and I wish I were at " home again in my own stall, or in my chim- " ney-corner with our Dorothy."

I 4

Wildgoose

Wildgoose faid, " he would not prevent his " returning home, if he defired it ; and would " pay him for the time which he had loft in " attending him : and then," continues he, " as you have been at no expence, you can " have no reafon to complain. Befides, you " own that Mrs. Cullpepper gave you fome " money ; and, perhaps, other good Chrifti- " ans may have been as liberal : and much " good may it do you !" Mr. Wildgoofe, however, faid, " he did not want to call him " to an account ; but only to make him fub- " mit with patience to the accidents which " might befall them in the Pilgrimage in " which he had voluntarily engaged to accom- " pany him. But come, Jerry," fays he, " I " believe we are not far from Cardiff, where " we fhall meet with better accommodations, " and (what is of more confequence) with a " Society of true Chriftians, which, I believe, " Mr. Whitfield eftablifhed there, when he " vifited the Principality of Wales."

Accordingly, in lefs than half an hour more, they came within fight of that handfome town ; which revived Tugwell's fpirits, who wifhed for nothing fo much as a cup of good

ale

ale and a flice of toafted cheefe, which, now he was in Wales, he hoped to have in perfec-tion.

CHAP. II.

Adventures at the Inn in Cardiff.

THE firft public-houfe, which the two Pilgrims came to, was one of thofe old, unfightly manfions, which, having been a well-accuftomed inn time out of mind, had had different conveniences added to it by different poffeffors; fo that it made, upon the whole, a comfortable, though very irregular, appearance. The houfe was at prefent very full; yet Tugwell contrived to get a nook in the kitchen-chimney, to fmoke his pipe and drink his ale (which was his principal concern); and Mr. Wildgoofe had a little parlour, near the ftable, for his breakfaft and his meditations.

As the Cambro-Britons are a nation of gentlemen, jealous of their honour, and impatient of affronts, they are engaged in frequent litigations: and there happened at this time to be fome Lawyers upon a commiffion at that inn.

I 5 Among

Among the reft, there was an eminent Attorney from Briftol, who came poft the day before, and whofe Clerk came into the kitchen, whilft Tugwell was eating a rafher of bacon, inftead of toafted cheefe, for his breakfaft.   As Jerry, by his Mafter's order, had been flily enquiring, " whether there were any Methodifts at Car- " diff;" the Lawyer's Clerk, interpofing, faid, " they had too many of them in Briftol; but, " thank God!" fays he, " two of them were " fhipped off for North-America yefterday " morning, juft as my Mafter and I fet out."— " For what?" fays one of the company!— " Why, one of the rafcals," fays the young Lawyer, " had been tampering with one of " our Aldermen's wives; and, by his curfed, " canting tricks, choufed the poor Alderman " out of an hundred pounds, or pretty near it, " to my certain knowledge."—" What was " the Alderman's name, then?" fays Tugwell, interrupting him, with an eager look.—"Why, " Alderman Cullpepper," fays the young Clerk. —" The Devil is a lyar, and fo are you," fays Tugwell; " for I know Alderman Cullpepper " better than you do; and I came from Briftol " but yefterday morning, as well as you."— " You know Alderman Cullpepper!" returns

the

the Lawyer. " What ! thou haſt been carried
" before him for a petty-larceny, I ſuppoſe."—
" I do not care a t—d for your *pretty laſſes*,"
ſays Tugwell; " but I know, that what you
" ſay is a curſed lye."—" Is it ?" ſays the
Lawyer. " I had it from his own ſervant;
" and I will pull thee by the noſe, if thou
" giveſt me the lye again," ſays he. " One
" of them pretended to be a man of fortune,
" forſooth, but wanted to borrow money of
" the Alderman ; and the other was a broken
" Cobler."—" How do you know I was a
" broken Cobler ?" quoth Tugwell. " If I
" was a Cobler, thank God, I never was
" broke."—" I will be hanged" (cries the
Lawyer, ſtaring in his face), " if thou art not
" one of them ; I have ſeen thy face in Briſtol.
" And the Alderman's ſervant told me one of
" them was a damned guttling fellow ; that he
" caught him in an intrigue with a pigeon-pye,
" behind the pantry-door, one morning be-
" fore dinner ; and that he had raviſhed above
" a dozen bottles of ſtrong beer in leſs than a
" week's time."—" I *trigue* with a pigeon-
" pye !" ſays Jerry; " it was nothing but a
" piece of pye-cruſt that the Cook gave me,
" and a little beſt drink to ſtay my ſtomach,

I. 6 " gentlefolks

" gentlefolks dine fo plaguy late. What!
" muft not a man, that preaches the Gofpel,
" eat and drink as well as other folks?"——
" Thou preach the Gofpel!" fays the Clerk;
" thou art more fit to fweep chimneys, or
" black fhoes, than to preach the Gofpel."——
As Jerry was going to retort with fome vehemence, this difpute might probably have proceeded to an affault and battery, if the young
Lawyer had not been called away by his Mafter.
And Mr. Wildgoofe, having now difpatched
his fhort breakfaft, fummoned Tugwell into
his little parlour, to know what intelligence he
had got about any Religious Society at Cardiff.
Jerry related to him, with fome indignation,
the report which the young Lawyer had brought
from Briftol: but Wildgoofe was lefs furprized
at the exaggerations of vulgar fame, than fhocked
at the fcandal which he and his friend Tugwell
had given, by accepting of Mrs. Cullpepper's
favours. And again expreffing his fufpicion,
" that Tugwell might have tafted more largely
" of her bounty than he cared to own," Tugwell wifhed " the Devil might fetch him, if
" he had had above half a guinea of *fich* a *mat-
" ter*, of any body's money, fince he came from
" home." Wildgoofe reproved him for his paf-
sionate

fionate exclamation; but his manner of expreffing himfelf, and his being fo touchy upon
the occafion, only confirmed Wildgoofe in his
fufpicions.

C H A P. III.

Wildgoofe holds forth to a Welfh Audience.

WHILST the two Pilgrims were debating
what courfe to take; as people at an
inn want to get rid of guefts when nothing
is going forwards for the good of the houfe;
the Drawer (or rather the Tapfter) came into
the room, to know whether *the gentleman called.*
Wildgoofe defired to pay for what they had
had; and, whilft he was doing that, enquired
of the Waiter, " whether there were any Me-
" thodifts, as they called them, in the town."—
" Yes, I believe there are," fays he, " more
" than are welcome: and we have got the
" famous Preacher Howel Harris in town at
" this time."—" Pray, who is he?" fays
Wildgoofe.—" Why, he is a young fellow"
(replies the Waiter) " that goes all over the
" country to revels and fairs, and preaches
" two

" or three times a day. He does a great deal
" of mischief amongst the country people;
" but I hope somebody or other will beat his
" brains out one of these days."

" What, I suppose, he spoils your trade, and
" would not have people get drunk, nor spend
" their time and money in wicked and idle di-
" versions?"— " I do not know," says the
Tapster; " I have nothing to say against the
" young fellow; I never saw any harm by
" him, not I: if you have a mind to hear him,
" I believe he preaches again to-night; and
" he lodges at a widow woman's, not far from
" our house."

As Wildgoose had heard Mr. Whitfield make
honourable mention of Brother Howel Harris,
he desired the Tapster to give them directions,
and went immediately and found him out. As
soon as they met, like true Free-masons, they
discovered each other's occupations, almost by
instinct; and, in the apostolical phrase,
Wildgoose gave Howel the *right hand* of fellowship.

When Howel Harris discovered Wildgoose's
inclination to harangue publicly, and that he
had already been employed by Mr. Whitfield,
he engaged to procure the Town-hall for him

that

3

that very afternoon; where, by trumpeting the fame of this new Preacher, he affembled above four hundred people. Wildgoofe held forth from the Judgement-feat; where he took occafion, without Judge or Jury, to *arraign* and *condemn* the whole race of Mankind. Many were very attentive; but fome mocked: and fome jolly fellows, who had been drinking at the inn, one of whom kept a pack of hounds in the neighbourhood, having had intelligence of Wildgoofe's intention by the Drawer, got a dead fox, and trailed him round the Townhall, and laid on his dogs to the fcent. The mufic of the hounds, and the noife of the fportfmen, was fo loud and vociferous, that it almoft drowned the voice of the Orator: and the chearfulnefs of the found had fuch a mechanical effect upon the minds of many of the Cambrians, that they ran out to join them; nay, Tugwell himfelf, in the midft of the preachment, could hardly refrain from giving them a *tallio*; but the recollection of the jeopardy he had been in, when he miftook the jack-afs for a ftag, checked his fpirit, and prevented him from deferting his ftation near his mafter, and joining the cry.

The

The Fox-hunters, however, were tired before the Preacher, who harangued for above an hour to a very attentive audience; and, what is remarkable, that part of the congregation feemed moft affected, and beftowed the moft hearty benedictions on the Preacher, who did not underftand a word of English. This, however, we ought not to attribute merely to affectation, but to the vehemence and apparent fincerity of the Orator, and the mechanical and infectious operation of an enthufiaftic energy.

It was towards evening before they difmiffed the affembly; and Wildgoofe, having been difturbed by the ftorm the preceding night, invited Howel Harris to fit an hour with him at his inn, where they fettled their plan for the next morning: and the two Pilgrims retired early to their repofe, highly fatisfied with the adventures of the day; which Wildgoofe faid (in the ftyle of the Journals), " was a day of " *fat things*;" to which Tugwell (applying it in a literal fenfe to his rafhers of bacon and Welfh ale) heartily affented.

CHAP.

CHAP. IV.

An unlucky Mistake.

THE house being very full (as was observed), our adventurers, being only foot-passengers, met with but scurvy lodgings. There was a room up five or six stairs, near the stable, with two miserable beds in it; in one of which the Hostler usually lay; and the other was reserved for the Drawer or Tapster, or any of the other servants, who might happen to be turned out of their own beds upon any extraordinary conflux of company; which was so much the present case, that the Hostler himself was turned out by Mr. Wildgoose, and forced to lie in the hay-loft; and Tugwell took up the other bed contiguous to his master.

The two travellers were but just got into their first sleep, when Nan the Cook, who happened to have a nocturnal intrigue with the Hostler, slipped up to Wildgoose's bed-side, and, calling the Hostler two or three times in a low voice, disturbed Wildgoose, who began to mutter some rapturous ejaculation in his sleep;

which

which Nan miſtaking for the amorous expoſtulation of an impatient lover, began to diſrobe
herſelf with great expedition; when, as ill
luck would have it, one of the Waiters, being
driven from his bed to make room for a
Lawyer's Clerk, came into the room with a
candle, and diſcovered poor Cooky half un-
dreſſed. She was an handſome, plump girl,
of about twenty-five; but, from the conſtant
heat and unctuous ſteams of the kitchen, her
complexion had more of the ruddy bronze of
an Italian peaſant than the pale delicacy of a
Northern beauty. However, ſhe was agreeable
enough to the groſs appetite of an Hoſtler, and,
as the Waiter imagined, to that of a Modern
Saint; for Wildgooſe, being now awaked (notwithſtanding the ſurprize which he expreſſed
at ſeeing ſuch company at his bed-ſide, and
the angry rebukes which he made uſe of for
this intruſion), the Waiter formed conjectures
by no means favourable to his virtue. Poor
Nan, pretending ſome miſtake, collected her
looſe robes, and hurried down ſtairs as faſt as
ſhe could; and the Waiter with her; at the
bottom of the ſtairs, they met the Hoſtler, who,
having heard ſome body go up into his uſual
apartment, ſuſpected the miſtake. The Waiter
told

told him, " that he had caught Nan in bed
" with the Methodist Preacher ;" which though
he did not entirely believe, yet it so far rouzed
his jealousy, that he heartily joined with the
Waiter in publishing the story the next morning.

CHAP. V.

An Apparition.

TUGWELL, being thoroughly fatigued,
and pretty well steeped in Welsh ale,
never waked during the above transaction : but,
about one o'clock, when the whole house was
quiet, and he had a little satisfied the importu-
nate demands of Nature, he was disturbed by
something at the feet of his bed ; when, opening
his eyes, he discovered by the twilight a most
diabolical figure standing upright before him.
It was about five feet high, of a grim aspect,
with eyes that glared like fire, a long beard,
and a monstrous pair of horns. " In the name
" of the Father, the Son, and the Holy Ghost,"
cries Tugwell, " what art thou ?"—The
Spectre made no other answer; but in an hollow
tone cried, " whare? whare?" Jerry, who
made

made no doubt but it was the Devil, and charitably suppofing that his bufinefs was with the gentlemen of the Law, replied, " that, if " he wanted the Lawyers, they lay in the beft " bed-chambers."—The apparition, as if he wanted no other intelligence, took his cloven feet immediately off the bed, and, like the Devil upon Two-Sticks, went ftumping down ftairs again, and difappeared.—Tugwell, however, awaked his companion in a great fright. " Mafter Wildgoofe! Mafter Wildgoofe!" fays he; " for God's fake awake: Lord have " mercy upon us!" fays he; " the houfe is " haunted; the Devil has juft appeared to me, " and is this moment gone down ftairs."— Wildgoofe, though in his difcourfes he frequently talked of the Devil and the power of Satan, yet did not really believe his vifible appearance to mankind. He took this opportunity, however, of reminding Jerry, " how free he had " made with the Devil's name about fo trifling " an affair as his receiving money upon the " road!"—", Lord have mercy upon us!" fays Tugwell; " to be fure, that is the reafon " of his appearance. Talk of the Devil, and " he will appear. I wifhed the Devil might fetch " me, if I had taken above half a guinea fince " we

"we came from *home*; and, to be sure, I
"have received three times as much from differ-
"ent people. But God forgive me, and de-
"fend me from the power of Satan, who is the
"father of lies."

Though Wildgoose did not trouble himself
about Jerry's perquisites, he was sorry to find,
that, after so much good instruction, he had
made no greater progress towards perfection.
He desired him, however, "to take another
"nap; for that the Apparition was only a
"dream, or a phantom of his imagination."—
"The *Fancy* of a *Magic Lanthern*!" says
Jerry; "no, no; I have seen a Magic Lan-
"thern at E'sham fair. It was no Magic Lan-
"thern," says Tugwell; "for I felt him, as
"well as saw him. He patted my legs with
"his cloven-feet; and he grew taller and
"taller, as I looked at him, till his head
"reached the ceiling; and I heard him walk
"down stairs: and, I am sure, the house is
"haunted by Evil Spirits; and I am for leav-
"ing this place as soon as it is day-light."

Mr. Wildgoose, who had been haunted by
the Flesh (in the shape of a fat Cook), as Tugwell had by the Spirit (in the shape of a Devil
as he thought), and not knowing what use
the

the Drawer might make of such an incident; being also impatient to get back to Gloucester, for reasons which the Reader may probably guess at; took Jerry's hint, and promised to set out by five o'clock, but desired Tugwell to compose himself till that time; which Jerry promised to do: and Mr. Wildgoose, being still much fatigued, took another nap.

Tugwell, however, could not sleep soundly; but, being waked again by the clock's striking four, and still haunted by the terrors of his fancy, he calls out again to his fellow-traveller, " Master Wildgoose! Master Wildgoose!" says he.—— "What is the matter now?" says Wildgoose.—— " O, nothing," says Jerry; " I " had only a mind to let you know, that you " have but an hour longer to sleep."—— " Pugh!" says Wildgoose; " but you need " not have waked me to tell me so."

The sun, however, began now to dart his first rays through the lattice, and discovered the ballads on the walls of their bed-chamber. People also began to move about the inn. Wildgoose therefore, and his friend Tugwell, thought it best to quit their beds, and decamp before the family were all stirring. Jerry, seeing his Master kneel down to his devotions,

just

juft caft up a fhort ejaculation ; but thought it more to his purpofe to examine the ftate of his wallet; which being pretty well exhaufted, he refolved to replenifh it with what he could get before they fet out.

As they came down into the ftable-yard, a great fhaggy he-goat, drawn by the fmell of Jerry's wallet, came running towards them; which Mr. Wildgoofe efpying, immediately obferved to his friend, " that was the Ghoft " which had appeared to him in the night."— Tugwell faid, " the Apparition had horns, and " a beard, like the goat ; but that he was as " tall as the houfe, and walked upright upon " two legs ; and, he was fure, it could be no- " thing but the Devil himfelf."——Wildgoofe did not ftay to convince him ; but, meeting with the Tapfter; who had waited on them the preceding night, paid him for what they had had ; yet not before Tugwell had drunk a pot of ale; and furnifhed his wallet with fome provifion for their journey.

CHAP.

CHAP. VI.

Reception by the Parson of Newport.

THOUGH Wildgoose was not very foli-
citous about the ludicrous turn which the
fervants at the inn might give to his adventure
with the fat Cook; yet, as he had promifed
Howel Harris to hold forth again that day at
Cardiff, and was unwilling to leave room for
any fufpicion in the mind of his friend, he
thought it proper to call upon him at his lodgings; and, though it was not yet five o'clock,
he found him already up, and at his meditations.

'As people who are good themfelves are not
apt to fufpect ill of others, Mr. Wildgoofe
found no difficulty in convincing his Brother
Howel of his innocence. He would have perfuaded Wildgoofe, however, not to quit Cardiff fo abruptly: but, when he found him determined, he immediately took his ftaff, and
fet out with the two Pilgrims towards Newport,
a confiderable town on the great road; where
he promifed to introduce Mr. Wildgoofe to the

4   Parfon

Parfon of the parifh, " who," he faid, " was a
" friend to their caufe, and had lent Mr.
" Whitfield his pulpit, when he lately vifited
" the principality of Wales."

They arrived at Newport before ten o'clock,
and accordingly waited upon the Doctor, who
received them in a polite manner, and told
them, " as he was perfuaded of Mr. Whit-
" field's good intentions, and knew alfo how
" fond people are of a new Preacher, and what
" an impreffion that very circumftance often
" made upon carelefs Chriftians, he had in-
" dulged his parifhioners, for once, in hearing
" fo famous a man; but that, in general, he
" did not at all approve of fuch irregular
" proceedings.

" I have already," continued the Doctor,
" found the ill effects of my complaifance to
" Mr. Whitfield. My own people, who are
" very well difpofed, and who were before
" entirely fatisfied with my plain doctrine,
" now, forfooth, give out, that I do not preach
" the Gofpel, becaufe I do not always harp
" upon the fame ftring, of the New Birth,
" Faith without Works, and the like. They
" alfo expect me to have private meetings
" two or three nights in the week, and com-

Vol. II.   K   " pliment

"pliment them with private expositions of
"Scripture, extempore prayer, psalm-singing,
"and what not; though, I really believe,
"if I were to give them the very same sermons
"in a private room, lighted up with candles
"like a play-house, the very novelty of the
"thing would content them for a while, as
"well as the best of your itinerant preachers."

Though the Doctor was not disposed to enter
into the views of our Spiritual Adventurers;
yet, as he kept an hospitable house, he entertained them with a good breakfast of coffee and
hot rolls; after which, Mr. Wildgoose and
Howel Harris parting with each other, the
latter returned to Cardiff; and Wildgoose,
with his fellow traveller, pursued their journey
to Gloucester.

CHAP.

CHAP. VII.

Au agreeable Solitude. An Holy Family, in the Flemiſh Style.

THOUGH Mr. Wildgooſe's principal view was to make the beſt of his way into the North, agreeably to Mr. Whitfield's deſtination; yet his more immediate object was, to reach Glouceſter as ſoon as poſſible, both to confirm the diſtreſſed Brethren there, and perhaps (in a ſubordinate degree) in hopes of another interview with Miſs Townſend before ſhe left that place, as ſhe daily expected to do. However, as both Mr. Whitfield in his Journals, and alſo Howel Harris, had repreſented the inhabitants of Wales as ſweetly prepared to receive the Goſpel (going frequently twenty miles to hear a ſermon); and as Howel had alſo informed him that there was a conſiderable Society eſtabliſhed at Monmouth, and had given him a letter to a ſubſtantial Tradeſman, who was the Chief Ruler of the Synagogue there;

K 2   for

for thefe reafons, Mr. Wildgoofe determined to take his route by the way of Monmouth.

Though Monmouthfhire is now in fome re-fpects an Englifh county, and is not fo moun-rainous as many parts of Wales; yet, to thofe whofe travels have never extended farther than Hammerfmith or Brentford, or a few miles round the Metropolis, the roads in this county would not appear quite fo level as a Kidder-minfter carpet.

Accordingly, the two Pilgrims, after two hours travelling, had now juft furmounted a Monmouthfhire mole-hill, and were come down into a romantic valley, on the banks of the Ufke, the coolnefs of which, as the fun was near its meridian, was extremely refrefhing. After winding along the river's fide for about half a mile, they came in fight of a pleafant village, at the foot of another hill, covered with hanging woods, which formed a beautiful amphitheatre; in the centre of which the Parifh-church, with its little fpire, rofe amongft fome old pine-trees; and the ruins of a Mo-naftery, near which the river formed a natural cafcade, fhewed that the place had formerly been dedicated to devotion and folitude. Wild-goofe could not but admire the fequeftered fituation;

tuation; and obferved, "that, if a true pri-
"mitive fpirit reigned amongft thofe people,
"they muft be the happieft of mortals."

The firft cottage they came to was a tolerably
neat one, and appeared the conftant refidence
of peace and tranquillity. A little wicket,
painted white, led through a fmall court to the
houfe, which was covered with honey-fuckles
and fweet-briar: the windows were glazed;
and the chimney rofe, with a truly ancient
Britifh magnificence, two feet above the thatch.

As the road divided at the end of the village,
Tugwell marched boldly up to the door, to enquire the way. On fo near an approach, however, they found, that Peace does not always
refide in a cottage; for their ears were faluted
with the confufed noife and fqualling of children; and a female voice, with a Welfh accent
(which is alway expreffive of anger), anfwered
Jerry, and bid him, "go about his bufinefs;
"that there was nothing for him; and that
"they had beggars enough in their own
"parifh."—Jerry replied, "that they did not
"come to beg, but to enquire the road to
"Monmouth."

A little curled-headed boy, with fhoes and
ftockings on, now opened the door; when they

K 3

heard

heard the forefaid female exclaiming, " Why
" do not you make hafte, and fcrape the
" bacon ? I wifh thofe books were all in the
" fire." Then, feeing Jerry's wallet on his
fhoulder, fhe cries out, " that they never
" bought any thing of Pedlars ; that her own
" father, who was a gentleman born, kept a
" creditable fhop at Newport ; and fhe would
" not encourage people who travelled about to
" the prejudice of the fair trader."

During this angry exclamation, Tugwell
and Wildgoofe had a full view into the kitchen ;
where, befides the boy that opened the door,
they faw four or five more, and the poor woman far advanced in her pregnancy. The
Mafter of the houfe, who was no other than
the Vicar of the parifh, was fitting down in
his band and night-gown; but fo far from
being idle, that his eyes, his hands, and his
feet, every limb of his body, and every faculty
of his foul, were fully employed : for he was
reading a folio, that lay on a table to the right ;
was hearing his little boy read, who ftood by
him on the left ; he was rocking the cradle
with his foot ; and was paring turnips.

As foon as he could difengage his attention
from this variety of employments, he rofe up,
and

and with a ftern air afked the travellers, " what
" they wanted?"——Wildgoofe repeated Tugwell's queftion, and defired to know, " which
" was the road to Monmouth?"—The Vicar
told them, " they were come near a mile out
" of their way ; but that, with proper direc-
" tions, they might eafily recover the right
" road."

Obferving Wildgoofe, however, upon a nearer
view, not to have the appearance of a common
tramper, he afked them, " if they would fit
" down *at the door,* and refrefh themfelves a
" little in the heat of the day? I cannot de-
" fire you to walk into the houfe," fays the
Vicar; " for, amongft the other comforts of
" matrimony, I have that of fitting my whole
" life in a wet room. My wife, as you may
" perceive, is a very good houfewife ; but
" (unfortunately for me!) fhe has taken it
" into her head, that a *wet* houfe and a *clean*
" houfe are the fame thing : fo that, having
" only one room to fit in, and that being
" wafhed every morning, it is confequently as
" you now fee it all the year round."

Mr. Wildgoofe faid, " he was forry to have
" given him the trouble of this apology, as
" he could not accept of his invitation."——

K 4

Tugwell,

Tugwell, however, [who feldom flighted an offer of this kind, faid, " he would be obliged " to the gentleman for a draught of fmall- " beer."——The Vicar, therefore, himfelf took a cup, ftepped to the barrel, which ftood in a little fhed, or *enclitical* pent-houfe, and brought Jerry, in a literal fenfe, fome *fmall*-beer, the refreshing liquor which he afked for.

C H A P.   VIII.

Ecclefiaftical Pride in the Diocefe of Landaff.

WHILST Tugwell was regaling him- felf with the forefaid potation, Wild- goofe repofed himfelf upon the bench at the door ; and, pointing to the ruins of the Mo- naftery, obferved to the Vicar, by way of chit- chat, " that there had been a Religious Houfe " in his parifh." — " Yes," fays the Vicar, " there *has been* a *Religious* Houfe in the parifh, " I believe ; but, I am forry to fay, it was long " before my time : for, I am afraid, at prefent " we have not one truly religious houfe in the " parifh."———" God forbid !" fays Wildgoofe ; " for, I dare fay, Sir, you do your duty " amongft

" amongſt them."—" Why," ſays the Vicar,
" I hope I do my duty as well as the genera-
" lity of my brethren; but am afraid, from
" particular circumſtances, it is not in my
" power to do much good in my pariſh."——
" How ſo, Sir?" replies Wildgooſe.—" You
" know, Sir," replies the Vicar, " that, at
" the Reformation, in Harry the Eighth's time,
" when the revenues of theſe Religious Houſes,
" by the Act of Diſſolution, were granted to
" the Crown, how ſlender a reſerve was made
" in general for ſerving the Pariſh-churches:
" Now, you muſt obſerve, Sir, that, after
" ſpending ſeven years in the Univerſity, and
" taking a Maſter of Arts degree, I am poſ-
" ſeſſed of a little Rectory, of about thirty
" pounds a year; and of this Vicarage, which,
" if I could make the moſt of it, might bring
" me in near twenty more: now, each of theſe
" preferments theſe poor people conſider as a
" *noble benefit*; and, though you ſee, Sir, in what
" way I live, yet, becauſe I am poſſeſſed of
" half a dozen ſpoons and a ſilver tankard,
" they envy me, as living in princely ſtate, and
" lording it over God's heritage; and, what
" is worſe, as my whole income in this pariſh
" ariſes from the ſmall tythes, becauſe I cannot
                    K 5   " afford

" afford to let them cheat me out of half my
" dues, they reprefent me as carnal and world-
" ly-minded, and as one who regards nothing
" but the good things of this life, and who is
" always making difturbances in the parifh.
" And this prejudice againft me prevents my
" doing that good amongft them which I fin-
" cerely wifh to do. One man has left his
" church, and walks three miles to a Metho-
" dift-meeting, becaufe I took one pig out of
" feven, as the Law directs; another has com-
" plained to the Bifhop of my extortion, be-
" caufe I would not take three fhillings and fix
" pence, in lieu of tythes for a large orchard,
" as my predeceffor had done. In fhort, Sir,
" here are two or three Diffenters in the parifh,
", who give out that all tythes are remnants
" of Popery; and would have the Clergy
" confider meat and drink as types and fha-
" dows, which ought to have been abolifhed
" with the Levitical Law."

" Well, Sir," fays Wildgoofe, " I cannot
" but think the fituation of a poor Vicar par-
" ticularly difagreeable, and that of the Clergy
" in general very much fo, in a temporal view.
" And, fince ' all malice (as a polite writer
" obferves) arifes from an oppofition of in-
" terefts,'

"terefts," I think it is pity, even upon that
"account, that things could not be put upon
"fome different footing between the Paftors
"and their flocks."——"Why," fays the Vicar,
"if it could be done without too great a con-
"fufion of property, I am fure, I fhould have
"no objection to it. And I have often thought,
"as things now are, to prevent that odium
"which every Incumbent muft bring upon
"himfelf, who is under a neceffity of dif-
"puting with his parifh the rights of the
"Church, a method might be contrived, to
"throw the burthen upon the Church itfelf,
"inftead of any particular Incumbent."——
"As how?" fays Wildgoofe.——"Why," fays
the Vicar, "that the Bifhop fhould be em-
"powered, by a fund levied in fome manner
"on the Clergy of the Diocefe (in propor-
"tion to their income), to defend the rights
"of any particular parifh; which, by refer-
"ence to fome neighbouring gentlemen, or
"other lenient methods, I fhould think might
"generally be done without much expence;
"and without involving a poor, miferable In-
"cumbent in continual fquabbles with his
"parifh, and preventing him from doing that
"good which probably he might otherwife do.

K 6   "But,"

" But," continued the Vicar, " there is no
" perfection to be hoped for in any human
" inftitutions; and, perhaps, an attempt to
" remedy the prefent might be attended with
" ftill greater inconveniences."

" I think," fays Wildgoofe, " there can
" be no greater misfortune than a mifunder-
" ftanding between a Minifter and his congre-
" gation; as it prevents all probability of the
" people's receiving any fpiritual improvement,
" if the Clergy were to take ten times the pains
" which they generally do.

" But pray, Sir," continues Wildgoofe,
" where is that Methodift-meeting, which
" you mentioned? Is it in our road to Mon-
" mouth?"——This enquiry confirmed the
Vicar in what he had before fufpected from
Wildgoofe's converfation, that he was a fa-
vourer at leaft of the Methodifts. He told him,
therefore, " that, if he wanted information of
" that kind, any of his parifhioners would
" give him ample fatisfaction; and would, upon
" occafion, leave the moft neceffary bufinefs,
" and walk twenty miles, to hear the extem-
" pore effufions of an illiterate Mechanic."

CHAP.

CHAP. IX.

Collects an Audience.

TUGWELL had by this time dispatched his small-beer, with a piece of bread and cheese and a pint of ale into the bargain ; for the Vicar's wife, having (through her mistake) treated him at first with undeserved asperity, was willing to atone for her rudeness by a superfluous civility, especially as, during her husband's conference with Mr. Wildgoose, Jerry had supplied his place, in rocking the cradle, paring turnips, and blowing the fire.

He was now, however, forced to leave the smell of the pot, being summoned to attend his Master, and proceed on their journey. In return for the Vicar's civility, Mr. Wildgoose took the liberty to exhort him, " to endeavour " the regaining his people's good-will, by some " little popular acts of beneficence, by relieving " the distressed, giving physic to the sick, or, " where he was obliged to exact his Easter " groats from any very poor families, to give " them a six-penny loaf in the place of its " and

" and the like innocent ſtratagems : but above
" all, Sir," adds Wildgooſe, " if the poor
" people had the true Goſpel earneſtly and
" affectionately inculcated into them, I am
" convinced, all theſe worldly conſiderations
" would entirely vaniſh ; and you would dwell
" together in unity and love."—The Vicar
thanked Wildgooſe for his good advice ; but
ſaid, " he had already uſed his utmoſt endea-
" vours to regain the good-will of his pariſhi-
" oners ; but was afraid nothing would ſucceed
" with people, who, to ſave a groat, would
" reſign their eternal ſalvation."—The Vicar
and the travellers then parted, with mutual good
wiſhes.

When the two Pilgrims came towards the
end of the village, they obſerved an old Taylor
ſitting on his board, with ſpectacles on his
noſe, and with more devotion than harmony
quavering one of Mr. Weſley's hymns. This
was hint ſufficient for Wildgooſe to make further enquiry about the Society of Methodiſts,
which the Vicar had mentioned. The Taylor
told them, " there was a weekly meeting at
" a village about three miles farther ; but that
" this was not the night on which the Preacher
" came."—Tugwell ſoon let him know, " that
" his

" his Master could supply that defect; and
" that, if it lay in their road to Monmouth,
" he would give them a word of exhortation
" that evening." Upon this, the old Taylor
leaped nimbly off his board; and, leaving a
suit of cloaths which he had promised to finish
that evening, said, " he would accompany
" them, if it were as far again;" and immediately ran and communicated this intelligence to a Blackfmith, his next neighbour,
who leaves the Farmer's horses half-shod, and
with like speed acquaints the Farmer's wife,
who was a zealous disciple of theirs. She,
slipping on her shoes and stockings, leaves her
cows unmilked, and her child dangerously ill
in the cradle; and, with half a dozen more,
who, upon spreading the alarm, had left their
several employments, joined the devout cavalcade *.

After many questions, who the gentleman
was, and whence he came, they set forwards,
and now marched chearfully along the valley;
Wildgoose making enquiry into the state of
their souls; and Tugwell entertaining them

* Such was the active zeal of the last Century :
" The Oyster-woman lock'd her fish up,
" And trudg'd away, to cry, No Bishop !"   Hun.

with

with some account of their adventures, and what he called persecutions, which they had undergone since they entered upon their Ministry.

The village whither they were bound, and where they soon arrived, was a considerable thorough-fare to Monmouth, and a populous place. The arrival of a new Preacher was soon spread about the neighbourhood; and there assembled, in half an hour's time, above two hundred people. When Wildgoose (being always desirous of attacking the Devil in his strong holds), having first refreshed himself with what the house afforded, held forth at the door of a little inn, being mounted on an horse-block, under a shady elm, which had long been sacred to rustic jollity and tippling, and thoroughly perfumed with the incense of ale and tobacco.

CHAP.

CHAP. X.

Miracles and flight Perfecutions.

AS foon as Mr. Wildgoofe began to harangue from the horfe-block, fome fervants belonging to the Squire of the village, who was a very orthodox man, and no friend to thefe fuperfluous acts of piety, began to make fome difturbance, and to beat a drum (that formerly belonged to the Militia); which at firft a little embarraffed the Orator: but he appearing much in earneft, and a majority of the company being more inclined to be attentive, they foon filenced thefe fcoffers; and Wildgoofe proceeded in his harangue.

A confiderable part of the congregation were feated on an orchard-wall, which faced the public-houfe; and, whilft Wildgoofe was declaiming with great vehemence, to an attentive audience, in praife of humility and felf-denial, and had juft affured them, " that he who humbled himfelf fhould be exalted," the whole wall on which they fat, being built of loofe ftones, fell flat to the ground, not one of them crying

crying out, or altering his posture; nor was
there the least interruption, either in the vehemence of the Orator, or in the attention of the
audience *.

But their tranquillity was soon after disturbed
by a phænomenon of another kind. A poor
fellow of a neighbouring hamlet (who used to
be always quarreling with his neighbours, but
who had been greatly affected by hearing Mr.
Wesley preach two or three times), came gal-
loping through the street, upon a little poney,
about the size of a jack-ass, hallooing and
shouting, and driving men, women, pigs, and
children, before him. He was without an hat,
with his long red hair hanging about his ears;
and, staring wildly, he rides up to Wildgoose,
crying out, " *Got* bless you! Master Wesley;
" hur is convinced of sin; and Got has given
" hur revelations, and visions, and prophecies;
" and has foretold, that hur shall be a king,
" and tread all hur enemies under hur feet †."

As the preaching was interrupted by this
poor man, some of the company told Wildgoose, " that he had been almost mad ever
" since he had heard Mr. Wesley preach."——
" Mad!" quoth Wildgoose; " I wish all that

* Ms. Wesley's Journal, 1740.   † Ibid.

" hear

" hear me this day were not only *almoſt*, but
" altogether as mad as this poor countryman.
" No," ſays he, " theſe are the true ſym-
" ptoms of the New Birth ; and he only wants
" the obſtetric hand of ſome Spiritual Phyſician,
" to relieve him from his pangs, from theſe
" ſtruggles between the Fleſh and the Spirit."
He then deſired thoſe who were ſtrong in
Faith to *wreſtle* in prayer for the poor En-
thuſiaſt : but he left them to wreſtle by themſelves ; and, without waiting for the event of
their application, galloped off again upon his
Welſh tit, hallooing and whooping, and as
frantic as before.

The preachment being ended, Tugwell, who
had been vaſtly taken with the ſinging of
hymns, which he had heard at Briſtol, thought
he might venture, in a country place, to exhibit a ſpecimen of his own talent at Pſalmody,
and give out the Pſalm ; though Jerry's voice
was as unharmonious as the falling of a fire-
ſhovel upon a marble ſlab. Both his muſic and
appearance, therefore, were ſo far from any
thing of devotion or ſolemnity, that the
Squire's ſervants, who had been awed to ſi-
lence by the vehemence of Wildgooſe's eloquence, could now hold out no longer. But
one

one of them began again to beat on the drum; and another difcharged two or three addled-eggs, which he had brought for the purpofe, at Tugwell's head; one of which flying directly into the aperture of Jerry's extended jaws, the unfavoury odour of the rotten eggs, and Jerry's refentment of the indignity offered to a man of his fancied importance, threw the whole congregation into confufion, and foon after difperfed the affembly.

Wildgoofe now began to reflect upon the efcape his audience had had from the tumbling wall, and to blefs God for what he fancied fo miraculous an atteftation to the truth of his Miffion. But the Farmer, who owned the orchard, confidered the affair in a different light; and, being no friend to the caufe, infifted upon an indemnification; and made poor Wildgoofe pay five fhillings and fix pence for dilapidations.

As the evening now came on, and the two Pilgrims were much fatigued with their early rifing and long walk, they thought it beft to fet up their ftaff at the public-houfe where they had preached. Tugwell, indeed, complained likewife of his having been pelted with addled-eggs. But his Mafter exhorted him, " to count it all joy, that he met with thefe
" divers

" divers temptations."—" Yes! great joy, in-
" deed," (quoth Jerry, in a pettifh mood) " to
" have rotten eggs in one's mouth, befides
" fpoiling one's cloaths, which I fhall not get
" fweet again this half-year."———Tugwell,
however, having got a rafher of bacon with his
eggs, and fmoked his pipe, was tolerably well
pacified ; whilft Wildgoofe went about, giving
fpiritual advice to different parts of the family :
and then the two friends retired to their repofe.

C H A P. XI.

Reception at Monmouth.

THE fun had been rifen about an hour,
when Wildgoofe fprang from his bed ;
and, it being likely to prove a very hot day,
foon rouzed his fellow-traveller, and fet out
for Monmouth. Tugwell, however, could
not leave an houfe of entertainment without
laying in fome provifion for the journey of the
day.

In all his travels, indeed, Jerry never wanted
a fubftantial reafon for making a good meal,
and filling his belly. In the morning, it was
a maxim

a maxim with him, to make fure of a good breakfaft, for fear they fhould not meet with a dinner. When dinner-time came, he pretended to be more hungry than *ordinary* that day, becaufe they had breakfafted before their time ; and at night he would obferve, that his journey had got him an appetite, and he never was *fo hungry* in his life before : though, if Wildgoofe had attended to his impertinence, he had probably made the like apologies every day fince they came from home.

As their road lay through fhady lanes or green meadows, they made pretty good fpeed ; and, without any thing worth recording, arrived at Monmouth early in the afternoon.

When Mr. Wildgoofe had found out the Tradefman, who was one of the Fraternity, to whom Howell Harris had given him letters of recommendation, he delivered his credentials. The man, cafting his eye over the letter, and finding Wildgoofe's bufinefs, received him at firft with fome little coolnefs ; and faid, " they " had of late had fo many *ftrange* Preachers, " that the credit of their Society had fuffered " greatly by their indifcretions." But, perufing the letter more carefully, and finding that Mr. Wildgoofe was no common itinerant,

4   but

but a man of fome fortune, and particularly delegated by Mr. Whitfield, he altered his ftyle, and, by way of apology for the fufpicions he had expreffed, related the following incident, which, he faid, had lately happened in that neighbourhood.

"A genteel young man," fays he, " came " down from London, who pretended to have " been a Preacher at one of Mr. Wefley's So- " cieties. He preached frequently at Mon-. " mouth ; and was well received in a gentle- " man's family in the neighbourhood, who " were religioufly difpofed. The gentleman " had a daughter, whom he was upon the point " of marrying, to great advantage, to a perfon " of fuperior fortune ; and the alliance would " have made two families extremely happy.

" This Itinerant, however, finding the young " lady rather indifferent in her affections for " this gentleman, who was, indeed, fourteen " or fifteen years older than herfelf, perfuaded " her, ' that fhe could not in confcience give " her hand without her heart ; and that it was " a kind of legal proftitution, to difpofe of her " perfon merely for the fake of a genteel fet- " tlement in the world, and the like ; efpeci- " ally to a man, whom he reprefented as *no* " *Chriftian,*

" *Christian*, becaufe he did not frequent their
" Religious Society.'

" In fhort, to prevent her yielding to the
" importunity of her friends, and even to the
" commands of her father, he perfuaded the
" young lady to march off with him into Ire-
" land, which was his native country, and
" where he had been a Journeyman-barber,
" and came to London in that capacity. But,
" by frequenting Mr. Wefley's Tabernacle
" for a few months, he had learned a few
" Scripture-phrafes, which, by virtue of a mo-
" deft affurance, he retailed to us in the country
" with great applaufe; though, it is to be
" feared, he had no true Faith, nor, indeed,
" any Religion at all in his heart. And this
" affair has brought a great fcandal upon our
" Society, and given too juft occafion for our
" adverfaries to blafpheme.

" However, Sir," continues the Tradefman,
" I hope a gentleman fo well recommended
" will contribute to retrieve our credit; and I
" will acquaint the Brethren with your arrival,
" and I hope you will this evening give a
" word of exhortation at my houfe."

Wildgoofe faid, " he would do his beft, as
" God fhould give him utterance; but would

" go

" go to the inn for an hour or two, to reſt and
" refreſh. himſelf, and about ſeven o'clock
" would meet the Society."

C H A P. XII.

A Stranger introduced to our Hero.

OUR two Pilgrims went to a ſecond-rate
inn; where, whilſt Wildgooſe was eating
ſome dinner in the parlour, Tugwell had pub-
liſhed the good qualities and preſent occupation
of his Maſter (over a pipe) in the kitchen.
This my Landlord had communicated to a
young Officer, who was quartered there, and
was lounging in the bar, and whom mine Hoſt,
for the good of the houſe, contrived, as often
as he could, to introduce to his company, to
make one at a bottle of wine, or a bowl of
punch.

This young man, however, had reaſons of
a more ſerious nature, for wiſhing to converſe
with a man of Mr. Wildgooſe's character and
pretenſions; and willingly conſented to the
Landlord's propoſal, of being introduced to this
devout Itinerant. As ſoon, therefore, as Wild-

had finished his flight repast, the Landlord told him, " that a young Officer, who was quar- " tered there, would be glad to drink a glafs " of wine with him."—Wildgoofe replied, " if " the gentleman defired it, he fhould be very " glad of his company; though he could not " promife to drink much wine with him."

Accordingly, there was introduced a tall, genteel young man, in his regimentals, who, throwing himfelf into a chair, and laying down his hat, with a fmart cockade, upon the table, unbuckled his fword-belt, and hurled his fword, with fome indignation, acrofs the room, crying out, " Thus let the weapons of " war perifh!"

Wildgoofe was a little difmayed at this fran- tic behaviour, and ftared at him with filent afto- nifhment; when the Man of war, looking wildly in his face, exclaimed again, with an air of diftraction, " Zounds! Sir, can you " give any relief to a foul that is haunted by " Furies?"—" Come, Sir," fays Wildgoofe, " do not defpair of God's mercy, whatever " your cafe may be: *Nil defperandum, Chrifto* " *duce.* Never be caft down, whilft you have " Chrift for your guide. I hope thefe are fa- " vourable fymptoms of the New Birth."— " New

" New Birth ! Sir : God forbid ! What ! be
" born again ! It is my misfortune that I
" ever was born at all.

" Why was I born with such a fenfe of Virtue,
" So great abhorrence of the finalleft Guilt ;
" And yet a flave to fuch impetuous Paffion !*"

As he was thus ranting in Heroics, Wildgoofe endeavoured to comfort him. " Come,
" Sir," fays he, " the firft ftep to converfion
" is, to be convinced of fin, as I hope you are :
" but, that I may be able to adminifter a pro-
" per remedy, let me know the nature of your
" difeafe."

" Well, Sir, if you have patience to liften
" to a long feries of irregularity and guilty plea-
" fures, I will give the beft account of myfelf
" that I can ; as it is always fome relief to the
" miferable, to lay open their griefs, where they
" can do it with fafety, as I am convinced I
" may to a man of your character, though
" you are a ftranger to me, and I have been
" guilty of murder ; nay, parricide, I believe ;
" adultery, and what. not."——" Well, well,
" fo much the better," fays Wildgoofe ;
" the more wicked and abandoned you have
" been, the more likely you are to be convinced

* Phædra and Hypolitus.

L 2

" of

" of fin. But pleafe to favour me with the
" particulars of your tranfgreffion."—The
ftranger then began the following narration.

CHAP. XIII.

The Adventures of Captain Johnfon.

"MY father," fays the Captain, " was a
" Merchant in London; where for fome
" years he carried on a confiderable trade:
" but, his health declining, and having only
" one hopeful fon (the wretch whom you here
" behold), he early in life retired from bufinefs.
" I was bred up at Weftminfter; and paffed
" through the fchool, I believe, with fome
" degree of credit; and was fent to the Uni-
" verfity with the character of an excellent
" Claffick.

" My father, hearing that my parts and
" fprightly genius had introduced me to the
" beft, that is, the moft expenfive company in
" the place, gave me very liberal appoint-
" ments; of which I made a very ungenerous
" ufe: for, inftead of improving myfelf in
" learning, or any valuable accomplifhment,
" the

" the only science, in which I made any pro-
" grefs, was that of a refined luxury and ex-
" travagance. And, in fhort, I was guilty of
" fo many irregularities, that although the
" Governors of the Univerfity were unwilling
" to expel me, yet they privately admonifhed
" my father to remove me from a fituation, of
" which I was fo far from making any proper
" ufe, that it muft foon prove equally deftruc-
" tive to my health and to my fortune.

" My father, who was too fond of me,
" thought it prudent to appear ignorant of my
" bad conduct; and wrote me word, ' that, as
" I had probably, by this time, made a tolera-
" ble proficiency in polite learning and philo-
" fophy, he was willing to finifh my education
" by letting me make the tour of Europe.'

" Accordingly, with no other Governor
" than an honeft Swifs, who ferved me in the
" double capacity of a Tutor and a Valet, I
" fet out upon my travels; to make my obfer-
" vations upon the laws and cuftoms, that is,
" to learn the vices and follies, of all the na-
" tions in Europe.

" During my ftay at Paris, I became inti-
" mate with an Englifh gentleman of fome
" diftinction, who was fettled with his family

L 3

" at

" at R——, in Normandy; whither, in
" confequence of a prefling invitation, I ac-
" companied him to fpend part of the fummer.
" As both he and his Lady were fond of
" company, I was foon introduced to people
" of the beft fafhion, of both fexes, in that
" province.

" There was a young Lady of great beauty,
" the wife of one of the Members of the Par-
" liament of R————, who was the moft
" frequently of our party. She had a gaiety
" in her temper, and a coquetry in her be-
" haviour; but not more than is common in
" the married women of that nation."—"Ah!"
cries Wildgoofe, " I am afraid, what you
" call by the foft names of gaiety and coquetry,
" are the lufts of the flefh, under a fpecious
" difguife; and that the French are an adul-
" terous and finful generation."—" I am afraid
" they are," fays the Captain; " and yet I que-
" ftion whether the inhabitants of this ifland are
" in that refpect much inferior to their neigh-
" bours on the Continent.—But to proceed in
" my ftory.

CHAP

CHAP. XIV.

The Adventures of Captain Johnson continued.

" LADY Ruelle (which was this Lady's
" name) had been something particular,
" as I fancied, in her behaviour to me. One
" evening, as we were walking in the gardens
" of my friend's house, with a large party of
" polite people, we found ourselves insensibly
" got into a private walk, detached from the
" rest of the company. 'Monsieur Anglois,'
" says Lady Ruelle, 'I long to see Londres,
" and wish I could meet with an opportunity
" of going over into England.'——As I thought
" this nothing more than unmeaning chit-
" chat, I imagined the most proper answer I
" could make her Ladyship was, 'that I should
" be very happy in shewing her our Metro-
" polis; and wished I might, some time or
" other, have that honour.'——She replied, with
" a sigh and languishing air, 'Ah! I wish,
" Monsieur, you were sincere in those profes-
" sions.'——The manner in which she spoke this
" surprized me a little; yet, as a man of gal-

L 4   " lantry,

" lantry, I could not but repeat my acknow-
" ledgments of the honour she did me, and
" offer to conduct so fair a Lady through the
" world, if she would permit me.   She then
" declared, ' that she was serious in her inten-
" tions;' but (as some company now walked
" towards us) said, ' she would explain herself
" more at large when she had an opportunity.'

" Lady Ruelle spoke no more to me that
" night : but, the next time we met, she took
" occasion to let me know, ' that her husband
" used her extremely ill ; that she had taken a
" fancy to me the first time she saw me ; and
" would put herself, and ten thousand pounds
" sterling, in money and jewels, into my hands,
" if I would accept of the offer.'

" Though I was startled at such a proposal,
" it flattered my vanity so agreeably, that,
" without reflecting on the consequences, I
" affected to receive with rapture and grati-
" tude so charming an overture.

" Not to be too minute in this detail,
" she had laid her plan ; and was determined, I
" found, to make her escape from a Masque-
" rade-ball, to which we were invited, near
" the suburbs of R———, the next night but
" one ; when she knew also, that her husband
                                    " would

" would be engaged the whole evening from
" home. I had time enough to deliberate up-
" on the wickedneſs and the danger of this
" expedition; the injury I was going to do
" the gentleman her huſband; and the diſho-
" nour I ſhould bring upon my Engliſh friend,
" who had introduced me to them : but, fired
" with the glory and gallantry of the action
" (as things then appeared to me), I was blind
" to every other conſideration.

" The next morning, therefore, I ſent my
" truſty Swiſs to Dieppe, with orders to get a
" veſſel ready to ſail at a minute's notice.

" On the night appointed for the Maſque-
" rade, about ten o'clock, Lady Ruelle ap-
" peared, dreſſed like a young gentleman, in
" a ſort of hunting ſuit of green and gold,
" and adorned with not leſs than five thouſand
" pounds-worth of diamonds, which ſhe had
" contrived to borrow of her huſband's rela-
" tions, under the pretence of this Maſquerade-
" ball.

" My ſervant had got the poſt-chaiſe ready,
" under a mount at the corner of the garden-
" wall : and, after ſupper, when the company
" were ſeparated into parties, Lady Ruelle and
" I eaſily contrived to give them the ſlip. I

L 5 " let

" let myfelf down; and the Lady, with great
" courage and alacrity, threw herfelf into my
" arms. I put her immediately into the car-
" riage; and we drove off, attended only by
" the Poftilion, and by my Swifs armed with
" a carbine, with great expedition, for Dieppe.

CHAP. XV.

The Adventures of Captain Johnson continued.

" AS the diftance, I believe, is not above ten
" leagues, or about thirty miles, we
" fhould probably have reached Dieppe with-
" out any interruption: but, upon our coming
" into a foreft, where the road divided, our
" Poftilion drove us fome miles out of the
" way, before he pretended to have difcovered
" his miftake. We had juft recovered our
" route, when we were overtaken by three
" men, well armed, who charged us to ftop, in
" the King's name. I had time to cock both my
" piftols: and my fervant, who was a bold
" fellow, bid them produce their credentials;
" which he received upon the end of his car-
" bine, but fhot the poor fellow dead upon
" the

" the fpot: the other two, like cowards as they
" were, fled with great precipitation; and
" we proceeded without any further moleftation
" to Dieppe. I there difmiffed the Poftilion,
" after prefenting him with the poft-chaife,
" which I had bought, for his faithful fervice;
" though it appeared afterwards that he had
" betrayed us.

" When we came to the harbour of Dieppe,
" we found the fhip, which my fervant had
" befpoken, riding at her cable's length, ready
" to fail. When we came on board, the
" Mafter of the veffel demanded our pafs-ports.
" I produced one for myfelf and for my fervant:
" But, when he found I had none for the
" young gentleman in green and gold, he fhook
" his head, and refufed to fail. I immediately
" cocked my piftol, and threatened to fhoot
" him through the head, if he perfifted in his
" refufal. He faid, ' I might do as I pleafed;
" but, if he carried off that young gentleman,
" whom he fufpected to be a perfon of
" confequence, he fhould be hanged the
" moment he returned to France.' I was
" not yet fo abandoned as to take away the
" life of an honeft man, upon fo flight a pro-
" vocation. After trying him again, there-
                    L 6.   " fore,

" fore, with a round fum of money, to no pur-
" pofe, we were forced to hire another chaife,
" and refume our journey by land; and pro-
" ceeded to Boulogne.

" Being come the next day within a few
" miles of that city, we were again overtaken
" by a man, whom, from his particular drefs,
" I knew to be an emiffary of the Police. He
" made a paufe, furveyed us all with an eager
" attention, and then made on, poft-hafte,
" towards Boulogue. As I gueffed his inten-
" tion was to apply to the Magiftrates of that
" place, and to take us into cuftody; I there-
" fore ordered the chaife to halt a little, and
" with Lady Rouelle's permiffion, got out,
" mounted my fervant's horfe, changed part of
" my drefs with him, and rode on full-fpeed, to
" reconnoitre how matters were likely to go in
" the city.

" When I came thither, I found the guards
" drawn out, and, with drums beating, pa-
" trolling the ftreets. I enquired for one of
" the principal inns; at the door of which I
" met by accident a young Englifhman, whom
" I knew to have been a fchool-fellow at
" Weftminfter, though he did not recollect
" me. He immediately told me, by way of

" news,

news, ' that the town was in an uproar, in expectation of seizing an English gentleman, who had carried off a Lady of the first quality from R———; and that he would be secured the moment the chaise came within the gates of the city.'

" Upon this intelligence, I immediately rode back as fast as I came; and, holding a council with my Swifs and the Postilion, we resolved to turn back out of the great road, and go to a small fishing-town, where, the Postilion told us, we had a better chance for hiring a vessel than at any of the more considerable sea-ports.

" When we came thither, I soon met with a petty commander of a fishing-boat, who, for a small sum of money, readily agreed to convey us the next day to Brighthelmstone. But I, foolishly enough, pulling out a purse of fifty louis-d'ors, which I offered him if he would sail immediately, at the sight of so extraordinary a sum, the fellow began to be alarmed; and then demanded our pass-ports, which he had never thought of before. I again produced those for myself and my servant; and shewed him a written paper, as a pass-port for the Lady. As the man could

" not

" not read, he said, ' he would go with us to
" the Curè, or Minister of the parish, to have
" the pafs-ports examined.'

    " The Curè had a gentleman-like appear-
" ance.   I took him afide, and told him, ' I
" would exprefs my gratitude to him, in any
" manner he fhould name, if he would affure
" the Mafter of the veffel, that the pafs-port
" was good, and prevail upon him to fail im-
" mediately.   The Curè replied, with a very
" ferious air, ' that he would not, for the
" whole world, abufe the confidence which
" his Parishioners placed in him, by deceiving
" them in a matter of fuch importance;' but
" very politely offered us an afylum in his
" houfe for that evening.   As we had no
" alternative, we gladly accepted the Curè's
" offer, that we might have time to confider
" what ftep was next to be taken.

CHAP.

CHAP. XVI.

The Adventures of Captain Johnson concluded.

" IT was now the third night since Lady
" Ruelle had been in bed; and, though
" she had slept a little in the post-chaise, she
" could not but be very much fatigued: with
" much difficulty, therefore, I prevailed on
" her Ladyship to go to bed. And having my-
" self sat up till about twelve o'clock with
" the honest Curè, I lay down, and had just
" composed myself, on a settee in the parlour,
" when I was awaked by an alarm, that the
" house was beset by the Officers of the Police.

" As we had reason to apprehend this, we
" had taken care to barricade the approach,
" and were determined to stand a siege. There
" was no way that they could attack us, but
" from a little garden near the parlour-window.
" I had armed my servant with his carbine,
" and myself with a pistol in each hand; and
" ordered him to keep his fire as long as pos-
" sible: but he, having a fair mark at one of
" them by the light of the moon, let fly, and

2

" killed

" killed him upon the fpot. But four more im-
" mediately marched up to the window, armed
" with blunderbuffes. I fired one piftol with-
" out effect. Upon which, they rufhing in
" upon us immediately, and threatening to
" fire if we did not furrender, it would have
" been madnefs to make any further refiftance.

" Lady Ruelle and I were feized, and put
" under a guard till near the morning; when
" we were placed back to back, and our hands
" bound behind us, in a fort of covered wag-
" gon; and in this manner conveyed to
" R———.

" Lady Ruelle, however, had the generofity,
" at my requeft, to flip her watch and a pearl
" necklace of confiderable value into my
" Swifs's hands; with which, by my orders,
" he contrived to make his efcape into his own
" country; and this circumftance was of
" great weight upon my tryal.

" I could not but remark one particular in
" Lady Ruelle, quite in the French ftyle.
" In the midft of her diftrefs, her eyes fwim-
" ming in tears, and when fhe could not but
" dread the confequence of this adventure,
" fhe runs up to the glafs, adjufts her head-
" drefs;

" drefs, and puts fome *rouge*, or red paint,
" upon her cheeks."

" Ah!" fays Wildgoofe, " thofe are the
" works of the Devil, the father of lies, and of
" every kind of deceit."

" Well," continues Captain Johnfon, " upon
" our arrival at R——, I was fent a clofe
" prifoner to the caftle. From thence I was
" foon brought to my tryal before the Parlia-
" ment of R——; and, as one of their Mem-
" bers was the injured party, fhould have been
" feverely dealt with, if they could have proved
" either the murders, or the rohbery, directly
" upon me: but, as my fervant was principal
" in the former, and alfo the only witnefs of
" the latter, and he had made his efcape; and
" as the Lady appeared rather more culpable
" than myfelf, having really feduced me; the
" chief party concerned feemed willing to
" drop the further profecution of the affair,
" efpecially as my good friend at R—— had
" made a very powerful application, by means
" of our Ambaffador, at the Court of Verfailles.
" So, after fome little confinement, I was
" difmiffed, with orders to quit the kingdom
" in three days time; with which I chearfully
                              " complied:

" complied : and the poor Lady was immedi-
" ately difpatched to a convent.

" Upon further enquiry into the caufe of
" this Lady's violent refolution, I found fhe had
" a fufpicion of the moft horrid kind, that her
" hufband, who was much older than herfelf,
" had an intrigue with her own mother."

Wildgoofe ftared with tokens of horror.
But, after fome paufe,—" Nay," fays he, " I
" wonder at nothing of this kind; for we are
" all by nature in the fame ftate with the Gen-
" tiles of old, ' given up to vile affections,
" unnatural lufts, and a reprobate mind, and
" to work all uncleannefs with greedinefs."

" Well," fays the Captain, " I am not yet
" come to the moft material part of my ftory,
" efpecially fo far as my own temporal intereft
" is concerned : for, on my arrival in England,
" I found my wicked courfe of life had con-
" tributed to fhorten my father's days, and my
" extravagance greatly diminifhed his fortune :
" for he was dead ; and, inftead of the afflu-
" ence which I had always depended upon, he
" left but about two thoufand pounds, to fup-
" port me and a mother, who is now but a
" middle-aged woman, though, from grief
" and

" and vexation, become very fickly and in-
" firm.

" Not to be tedious, I found myfelf in im-
" mediate poffeffion of no more than five hun-
" dred pounds; with which I purchafed a
" Lieutenancy, and am now doing penance in
" country quarters, ftrutting about in my red
" coat and cockade, but really a prey to me-
" lancholy, and tortured with reflecting upon
" thofe vices which have brought me fo early
" in life to this wretched fituation."

C H A P. XVII.

A Temporary Converfion.

CAPTAIN Johnfon having finifhed his narration, Mr. Wildgoofe bid him, " not de-
" fpond; that Providence often brought about
" our converfion by fevere trials; and that it
" was a maxim with them, ' The blacker the
" Sinner, the brighter the Saint.' But," fays
he, " I am going to meet a Society of true
" Chriftians; where, I make no doubt, you
" will find thofe, who have been as wicked as
" yourfelf, now full of peace and joy. And,
                              " I affure

"I assure you, Sir, I have heard Mr. Whit-
"field often say, ' that he had rather preach
"to a congregation of Publicans and Harlots,
"or what the world may call Whores and
"Rogues, than to a set of mere nominal
"Christians, or good sort of people, as they
"are called, who flatter themselves that they
"need no repentance."

The Captain said, "that, although he should
"be called a Methodist, and was really invited
"to dance at a sort of Welsh assembly, he
"would accompany Mr. Wildgoose, by his
"leave, to their Society."

Accordingly, having sat together till near
seven o'clock, Mr. Wildgoose took Captain
Johnson with him, attended by his friend
Tugwell, to the Tradesman's house; where
he found a pretty large congregation, assembled
in an upper room, over his warehouse in the
garden.

Wildgoose harangued upon the usual topics
with great pathos; and, as several people round
him sighed and groaned, and even wept, the
Captain found himself variously affected, sometimes inclined to laugh, at other times to cry:
but what he found most contagious were, the
tears of a very pretty girl, a Grocer's daugh-

ter,

ter, who fat near him, with whom the Captain would have been glad to have compared his feelings and experiences; for, though he was probably fincere in the compunctions which he difcovered in converfing with Mr. Wildgoofe, yet, when the paffions have got ftrength by long indulgence, they are not immediately to be fubdued, but are apt again to take fire upon approaching a tempting object : nay, as twenty or thirty of the moft zealous of them were defirous (according to a common practice) of fpending the night in the Society-room, the Captain ftayed amongft them for fome time, and was thought to have been made a complete convert by this young female difciple.

As Mr. Wildgoofe, however, had been up early in the morning, and was fatigued with the toils of the day; he himfelf, about eleven o'clock, lay down upon a bed that was offered him by the pious Tradefman; and Tugwell's devotion was fo far from being enthufiaftic this evening, that, before Wildgoofe had done preaching, he was fallen afleep in the corner of the room.

But, about two in the morning, Mr. Wildgoofe was waked * by a confufed noife, as if

* Mr. Wefley's Journal, 1739.

a number

a number of men were putting to the fword. He went up into the Society-room, where the people had worked themfelves up to fuch a pitch of religious phrenzy, that fome were fallen proftrate upon the floor, fcreaming, and roaring, and beating their breafts, in agonies of remorfe for their former wicked lives; others were finging hymns, leaping and exulting in extafies of joy, that their fins were forgiven them.   Amongft the reft, there was a little boy*, of three years old, who had caught the infection, and acted the Sinner with as much appearance of con-trition as the beft of them.   The uproar in-creafed when Wildgoofe came into the room, aud began to pray with them: but Nature, having now been ftrained to its height for fome hours, fubfided into a calm.   Wildgoofe, there-fore, difmiffed them with a fhort exhortation, and lay down again till the morning, leaving Tugwell to finifh his night's reft, where he had begun, upon fome hop-facks in the corner of the affembly-room.

The Captain (he found upon enquiry) about eleven o'clock had conducted home the Grocer's daughter, whofe father and mother had fent for her; for, although they indulged her in going

* Journ. 1738.

(with

(with some other young people) to the Meeting, they did not approve of those late nocturnal vigils, which were frequently solemnized by the warmer devotees.

Amongst others in this devout assembly, there was a substantial Miller's wife, who lived about a mile out of town, that was more zealous than any of them. She intreated Mr. Wildgoose, " if possible, to come home to her, and " give her some private consolation; as Mr. " Whitfield, Mr. Wesley, and other gentle- " men," she said, " had sometimes done."— When Wildgoose found she lived partly in the road towards Gloucester (whither he intended to direct his course in the morning), he promised the good woman to call and take a breakfast with her about seven o'clock.

CHAP. XVIII.

A warm Breakfast, concluded with cold Sause.

JERRY Tugwell, having been disturbed by the uproar in the night, no sooner met his Master in the morning, than he began to vent his indignation with some warmth against the

good

good peop'e of Monmouth. " Gad-zookers !"
fays he, " thefe Welfh people are all mad, I
" think ; I never heard fuch rantipole doings
" fince I was born ; a body can not fleep
" o' nights for 'em."

" Ah ! Jerry," replies Wildgoofe, " this
" is a glorious time ! thefe are the triumphs
" of Faith ! thefe are the true fymptoms of
" the New Birth ! People are never nearer to
" the Kingdom of Heaven than when they are
" *mad,* as you call it ; and have never better
" reafon to hope for Salvation, than when they
" are ready to hang and drown themfelves.

" But come, Jerry," fays he, " a poor
" fifter is labouring under the pangs of the
" New Birth, and wants our affiftance. We
" muft walk a mile or two before breakfaft."—
" Walk a mile or two before breakfaft !" fays
Tugwell ; " why, I had no fupper laft night ;
" and my ftomach is fo empty, that I can
" hardly walk at all without my breakfaft. If
" the young woman is in *labour,* fhe has more
" need of a midwife than our affiftance."

As Wildgoofe, therefore, was taking leave
of the Tradefman, Tugwell got a piece of bread
and cheefe, and a cup of ale ; and then they
went to the inn, to call upon the Captain :
but,

but, hearing that, notwithſtanding his fancied converſion, he had gone from the Religious Meeting to the profane dancing aſſem-
bly, and had not been come to bed above two
hours, the two Pilgrims ſet out upon their
expedition.

When they came to the mill, which was
not above a mile out of town, they found a
good breakfaſt prepared for them by their kind
hoſteſs, the Miller's wife; for, the Miller
having ſet out early in the morning, the good
woman, who thought ſhe could not do too
much for ſuch good people, had got ſome
cakes baked and buttered, and all other re-
quiſites for a comfortable *dejeuné*. And in
this manner, with the addition of ſome godly
converſation, the poor woman frequently regaled herſelf; and always found herſelf more
happy, than in the ſurly ſociety of her mo-
roſe huſband; which happineſs ſhe aſcribed to
the power of religion, rather than to, its more
probable cauſe, the variety it introduced, and
to the comfortable ſoothing doctrine of being
ſaved by Faith without Works.

And, indeed, the Miller, though fond of
his wife (who was much younger than himſelf,
and a tolerably handſome woman), and un-

willing

willing absolutely to forbid her frequenting
these pious Meetings; yet, as he was often,
by this means, deprived of his conjugal claims,
and the company of his spouse, who (according to the old Liturgy), ought to have been
buxome both at bed and at board, he was generally
out of humour upon these occasions; and
could not forbear expressing his disapprobation
of the many Itinerants which came to the
house, amongst his workmen and servants.
These fellows, therefore, who were more in
their Master's interest than in that of their
Mistress, laid a plot, which they knew would
not displease their Master, but which, if he had
been at home, he probably, out of regard to
his wife, would not have suffered them to execute.

The nearest way, for the two Pilgrims to return into the great road, was through a mea-
dow, into which they must pass over the Mill-
stream, by a narrow plank, which was laid
across it. This plank the fellows contrived
to saw almost in two, on the under-side.
When, therefore, the travellers had taken
their leave of the Miller's wife, Wildgoose,
leading the way, marched foremost nimbly
over the bridge; which, though it cracked,
did

did not entirely break down till he was landed ; and Tugwell came upon the middle of it, who, being a heavy-a—d Christian, and moreover encumbered with his loaded wallet, fell plump into the stream, bawling out for help, to the no small diversion of the spectators. The men ran, however, to Jerry's assistance with a feigned concern, and dragged him out of the water; but took care that he should first be dipped into it considerably above the waist.

- The fright and the surprize at first took away Jerry's voice, that he could not vent his indignation. One of the fellows handing him up his wallet, " 'Sblood ! Honesty," (says the man) " thou hast but just *saved thy bacon.*"— " What the Devil do you mean by saving " my bacon ?" says Tugwell. " It is nothing " but my Master's Bible and some good books " in my wallet." The fellow, indeed, by that proverbial expression, only alluded to the narrow escape Jerry had had ; but spoke the literal truth by chance : for the Miller's wife, it seems, out of her great regard to the godly, had offered Tugwell a piece of bacon, of about five or six pounds, which, for fear of accidents, Jerry (unknown to his Master) had accepted of, and stowed in his wallet; and the con-

sciousness

scioufne's of his greedinefs now made a difcovery, which the Miller's men perhaps would
not otherwife have fufpected.

One of the fellows afked Tugwell, with a
fneer, " if he would go back and dry himfelf,
" and have another difh of tea." But Tugwell, muttering fome threats, trudged after
his Mafter as faft as he could, equally afhamed
to be thus out-witted, and vexed to be wetted
to the fkin. And, upon Wildgoofe's exhorting him " to fuffer tribulation with pa-
" tience;" Jerry replied, in great wrath; " that
" he did not care who fuffered tribulation,
" fo that he was got fafe home again in his
" chimney corner."

C H A P. XIX.

A feafonable Relief.

THEY had now proceeded about three
miles on their journey from Monmouth;
when they came to a confiderable brook, which
ran at the foot of a fteep hill, covered with extenfive woods. There was a foot-bridge to
pafs over; but, the rivulet being fwelled by a
violent

violent thunder-storm which had fallen in the
night, they could not possibly approach the
bridge. Being obliged, therefore, to halt, they
fat down upon the bank, and were deliberating
what courfe to purfue; when Tugwell began
to complain of being very chill, and of the
head-ach, and faid, " he was certainly going
" to have a fit of the ague, and fhould not be
" able to go any further." He then heavily
bemoaned himfelf, and faid, " if he were at
" home, Dorothy would carry his water to the
" *Cunning Man,* who would caft a fpell, or
" fend him a bottle of *ftuff,* which would cure
" him after the third fit; or elfe Madam Wild-
" goofe would fend him fome * *Higry-pigry,*
" which would ftop it at once."

Whilft they were thus engaged, Tugwell
complaining, and Wildgoofe endeavouring to
encourage him by the examples of Martyrs,
Saints, and Confeffors; they obferved a horfe
grazing at fome diftance by the wood-fide, with
a fort of pack-faddle upon his back, and the
bridle hanging loofely between his legs. Having
now waited near a quarter of an hour, and
nobody appearing to whom the horfe might
probably belong; Mr. Wildgoofe obferved to

* Hiera Picra, or Sacred Bitter.

M 3

his

his friend, " that Providence * had certainly de-
" livered this horfe into their hands, to pro-
" mote the great work in which they were
" embarked."—Tugwell, however, for more
reafons than one, objected to taking an horfe,
which certainly did not belong to them.—
Wildgoofe owned, " it was not lawful to fteal,
" or even to covet our neighbour's ox, or his
" afs, or any thing that does not belong to us."
" But," fays he again, " we are commanded to
" ufe all diligence in our power; which muft
" fignify, the ufing all the means, to compafs
" any end, which falls in our way. Now, we
" fhall certainly make more fpeed on horfe-
" back than on foot; and, therefore, we may
" lawfully, I think, make ufe of this horfe,
" which is thus providentially ready bridled
" and faddled for our ufe."

To this Tugwell made two objections;
firft, " that, perhaps, the water was too high
" for them to ride through;" and, fecondly,
" that he could not ride, having never been
" on horfe-back fince he was ten years old."

Wildgoofe replied, " that, as Jerry was
" afraid, he himfelf would firft ride through,
" and, if it were fafe, would return and take

* Journal, *paffim*.

" Jerry

" Jerry behind him, and convey him to the
" next inn; and, by putting him into a warm
" bed, he did not doubt but he would foon
" be as well as ever.

" But," continues Wildgoofe, " to make
" fure of the lawfulnefs of what we are about,
" we will have recourfe to our Bible, as Mr.
" Wefley and Mr. Whitfield have often
" done." Upon opening it, therefore, they
dipped upon that paffage where the difciples
were ordered to bring the afs's colt, for their
Mafter's triumphant entry into Jerufalem.
This Wildgoofe confidered as a cafe in point,
and decifive in their favour. He went therefore to catch the horfe, when he fpied alfo an
old blue great coat thrown into the ditch;
which it puzzled him yet more to account for.
But, as he intended to leave the horfe at the
firft inn they came to, he thought it beft to
take the coat alfo, and wrap up his companion,
who was ftill fhivering with cold.

Upon fearching the pocket of the great coat,
they found in it an old crape hat-band, a
pocket knife, and an iron tobacco-box.

Wildgoofe now leaped upon Rofinante;
and, riding boldly into the brook, found it
barely fordable (as the flood was abating),

M 4.   which

which it probably had not been in the morn-
ning, when it was at the higheſt. He, therefore, returned, and with ſome difficulty
dragged Jerry up behind him, wrapped in the
great coat; and, thus croſſing the brook,
they marched ſlowly up the hill, through a
deep and rough hollow way. They deſcended
the hill again; and, after riding about a mile
further, came to a little village, where meeting
with a public-houſe, they ſtopped, hung
the horſe at the door with the great coat
upon the pad, and put Jerry into a warm
bed, who deſired a little treacle-poſſet, which
threw him into a perſpiration, by which he
ſoon recovered his uſual vivacity.

CHAP. XX.

Taken up upon Suſpicion.

WHILST Wildgooſe was waiting in a
ſort of little parlour for his fellow-traveller's recovery, my Landlord had prevailed
upon him, as his beard was near a week's
growth, to ſubmit to the operation of a Barber,
who had juſt ſhaved my Landlord. The ope-
rator

rator had juſt finiſhed one ſide of Wildgooſe's
face, when five or ſix men ruſhed into the
houſe, armed with clubs, pitch-forks, and an
old gun; which was part of the hue-and-cry
raiſed by a Farmer, who had been robbed that
morning, in his way to the fair above-men-
tioned, by a man upon the very horſe which
Wildgooſe and his friend had made uſe of.

They enquired where the perſon was, to
whom the horſe at the door and the blue great-
coat belonged. My Landlord pointed to Wildgooſe, as he was ſhaving in the next room with
his back towards him. The fellows ſurveying
him pretty narrowly, one of them cried out,
" Aye, that is he; I can anſwer to him; he
" was a tall, thinniſh man, juſt his ſize." They
then began diſputing, who ſhould go firſt into
the room, and ſeize the villain. The Farmer
that had been robbed ſaid, " it was the Con-
" ſtable's duty to apprehend the criminal."——
The Conſtable ſaid, " he would take him
" before the Magiſtrate, but would not ven-
" ture his life upon other people's buſineſs."——
A Butcher, who was amongſt them, made ſigns
to the Barber, to cut his throat, without any
more ceremony. But, the honeſt Barber either not
underſtanding their hints, or having more ſenſe
M 5 than

than to comply with them, the Farmer's fon
who had been robbed, a young man about fe-
venteen, fnatched the gun out of the hands of
one of them, and immediately feized Wildgoofe, in the King's name, for *villoneoufly*
robbing an honeft Farmer that morning upon
the King's highway. And, without fuffering
Wildgoofe to make any defence, or the Barber
to finifh the other fide of his face, they were
hurrying him immediately before a Juftice of
Peace; when my Landlord informed them,
" that there was another of them, who came
" with the horfe, and who wore the blue
" great coat which was left upon the pack-
" faddle."

At that inftant, Tugwell finding himfelf
pretty well recovered, and his returning appetite putting him in mind that he had acted the
fick man long-enough, he was juft come down
into the kitchen. And the Landlord tipping
the wink, the Conftable feized him alfo by the
collar, in the King's name. " What the
" pox is the matter now!" fays Tugwell;
" what do you collar me for, and be hanged ?"
—" Only for ftealing an horfe, and robbing
" upon the high-way," fays the Conftable.
The man who had been robbed feeing Jerry
feized,

feized, and hearing his voice, cried out again; " Aye; that is the very rogue that robbed " me; I can fwear to his voice." And he now faid, " it was a fhort thick-fet fellow;" though he had before given juft the contrary defcription of him.

The gentlemen of the hue-and-cry were going to tie the culprit's hands behind them, and their legs under the horfe's belly, in order to carry them before the Juftice; but mine Hoft obferving, " that there were enough to " guard them without that precaution," they fet them both upon the horfe as they had been before: and thus they marched with them near four miles, to one Mr. Aldworth's, on the borders of Herefordfhire; Tugwell (according to cuftom) bewailing his misfortune; and Wildgoofe adminiftring his ufual topics of confolation.

M 6. GHAP.

CHAP. XXI.

A Justice, and a Justice of the Peace.

MR. Aldworth was an opulent country gentleman, and a very worthy Magistrate. His way of living gave one the truest idea of that hospitality for which the English nation was formerly distinguished. I mean not in the days of Queen Elizabeth, when even the Ladies breakfasted upon toast and metheglin, or cold beef (which days I consider, in that respect, as somewhat barbarous and semi-gothic); but of that hospitality which subsisted amongst our gentry till the Revolution, and continued in some measure to the days of Queen Anne and George the First: when, instead of being tantalized with a dozen of French dishes (which no Frenchman, however, would ever taste), and stared at by as many French servants, dressed better than yourself or their own Master; instead of being dragged out, the moment you have dined, to take a walk in the shrubbery, and wonder at his

Lordship's

Lordship's *bad* taste, and then frightened away with the appearance of cards and wax candles; instead of this refined luxury, I say, you were sure to find at Mr. Aldworth's, a ham and fowls, a piece of roast beef, or a pigeon-pye, and a bottle of port-wine, every day in the week; and, if you chose to spend the night at his house, a warm bed, and an hearty welcome.

This hospitable temper and friendly reception general y filled Mr. Aldworth's table; and none of his old acquaintance, who came within ten miles of him, ever thought of lying at an inn, when he was in the country; which, indeed, unless any extraordinary business called him to London, was usually the whole year.

The reader will pardon this tribute to such primitive merit; which, indeed, serves also to render more probable an incident in the sequel.

Mr. Aldworth was at dinner, with some company, when the culprits and their cavalcade arrived at the door: they were, therefore, ordered into a little summer-house, at the corner of the garden; where the Squire used both to take a sober glass with a particular friend,

or

or to diſtribute juſtice amongſt his neighbours
with equal wiſdom and impartiality;

" And ſometimes counſel take, and ſometimes wine."

.. Amongſt other company now at Mr. Aldworth's, there was one Mr. Newland, a young
man of fortune; who, inſtead of going to the
Univerſity, to Paris, or even to the Temple,
to ſtudy the Laws of England, had been edu-
cated under an eminent Attorney in the country, and conſequently was a rigid obſerver
of the letter of the Law; and, having but
lately been put into the Commiſſion, he was
impatient to act the Magiſtrate, and flouriſh
his name at the ſide of a Mittimus.

Mr. Newland, therefore, having paid a proper compliment to the ſecond courſe, by ſwal-
lowing a leg and wing of a ducklin, and a
plate of green peaſe; and having drunk hob-
or-nob with a young Lady, in whoſe eyes he
wiſhed to appear a man of conſequence; he
hurried out into the ſummer-houſe, where
he made the Clerk immediately ſwear the
evidence, and take the depoſitions; over
which as ſoon as young Newland had caſt his
eye, and had ſurveyed Wildgooſe's face, half-
ſhaved (which he took for a diſguiſe); " Well,
" you raſcal," ſays he to Wildgooſe, " what
" have

" have you to say for yourself, guilty or not " guilty ?"——" Ah !" says Wildgoose, shaking his head, " I am but too *guilty*: God forgive " me! and am laden with iniquities."— " There," says the young Magistrate to the Clerk, " you hear he confesses it." He then bid the Clerk fill up the Mittimus; and he would sign it, without giving Mr. Aldworth the trouble of leaving the company.

C H A P. XXII.

A Friend in Need is a Friend indeed.

WHILE this was transacting, however, the good old Gentleman, being aware of his young Colleague's precipitate temper, came out, with the napkin tucked in his button-hole, and began to enquire a little into the circumstances of the affair. It appeared from the deposition, " that the Farmer had been " robbed of seven guineas that morning about " five o'clock, by a man upon that very horse, " and in that blue great coat, with a black " crape over his face, and armed with that " very long pocket-knife;" all which were
found

found in Tugwell's and his Master's pos-
seffion.

Mr. Aldworth, however, notwithstanding
these particulars, and the suspicious circum-
stance of Wildgoose's double-face (which, indeed, the Landlord soon cleared up), saw an
appearance of honesty in Wildgoose, and even
in his friend Tugwell; which inclined him to
think more favourably of them than Mr.
Newland had done. He, therefore, asked
Wildgoose, " what account they could give of
" themselves, whence they came, and whither
" they were going ?"——Wildgoose replied,
" that they had come from Gloucester, and
" had been at Bristol upon a business of
" consequence; but, for some particular rea-
" sons, had been obliged to return through
" Wales and Monmouthshire."

This account appearing somewhat incohe-
rent, Mr. Aldworth asked, " how they came
" by that horse and the great coat ?" Which
Wildgoose explained to him; and added,
" that probably the person, who committed the
" robbery, finding the brook not fordable in
" the morning, on account of the flood, had
" made his escape into the woods on foot.
" But, however that might be, though he
                                    " owned

" owned himself guilty of many other crimes
" in the fight of God, yet he was never guilty
" of robbery; and that he himself and his
" fellow-traveller were at breakfast at a Mil-
" ler's, near Monmouth, at seven o'clock that
" morning; and that he could bring an hun-
" dred people to witness, that he had preached
" at a Religious Society at Monmouth the
" preceding night."

" O, ho!" says Justice Newland, " are you
" at that sport? Your preaching at Mon-
" mouth last night does not prove, that you
" did not rob upon the highway this morning.
" Many of these Itinerant Preachers have done
" the same."

" Well, well," says Mr. Aldworth, " let
" us suspend our judgment till we have en-
" quired more into this affair. Where is your
" proper place of residence?" says he to Wildgoose; " and what trade or profession are you
" of?"—Upon Wildgoose's answering, " that
" he lived in the North part of Gloucester-
" shire;"—Mr. Aldworth said, " they should
" then probably get some light into his cha-
" racter, and give him an opportunity of
" clearing himself, by a Gentleman who was
" then in the house. Here!" says he to a servant,

vant, " defire Mr. Powel to ftep hither a
" moment."

Wildgoofe, finding himfelf oddly affected
at the name of Powel, though he did not immediately know why, changed colour; which
Juftice Newland obferving, winked upon Mr.
Aldworth with a fagacious nod. " But," fays
he, " this old rafcal is the principal; and I
" fufpect he is returned from tranfportation,
" for I remember his face at Monmouth af-
" fizes feven years ago, when I was firft Clerk
" to Mr. Traverfe."

Tugwell was going to clear himfelf of that
afperfion, when Mr. Powel appeared, who
was no other than the Parfon of the parifh
where Mr. Wildgoofe lived, and whom we
mentioned as the accidental caufe of Wildgoofe's difguft with the world. Mr. Powel
was returning from a vifit to his friends in
Wales; and had made Mr. Aldworth's houfe
a convenient ftage by the way.

The mutual aftonifhment of Mr. Powel and
the two Pilgrims, at meeting each other in this
place, and on fuch an occafion, was propor-
tionable to the improbability of fuch a rencounter.

Mr.

Mr. Powel expressed his concern at seeing his old neighbours in such a situation; but could hardly forbear laughing, to see one side of Wildgoose's face close-shaven, and the other with a beard half an inch long.

Mr. Wildgoose was in some confusion at this unexpected meeting with Mr. Powel, as he did not like to be obliged to a man, against whom he had conceived so violent a prejudice; and also was afraid of being disappointed, in what he really wished for, the being persecuted for the Gospel's sake, as he esteemed it, and (like honest John Bunyan) the singing of Psalms in a Gaol.

Upon Mr. Powel's telling him, however, "that "his mother had been greatly affected with his "absence, and had had a dangerous fit of sick-"ness," he found some symptoms of humanity revive in his breast; an involuntary tear rose into the orbit of his eye; and he even expressed some hope, that she was quite recovered.

But, as for Tugwell, his joy was excessive, and quite sincere, at meeting the Vicar of his parish, for whom he had always a thorough reverence and esteem.——— "God in Heaven "bless you, Master Powel!" cries Jerry: "how does our Dorothy do, and my poor "dog

" dog Snap, and Madam Powel? Ah! Ma-
" ster, we have been all the world over, by sea
" and by land, over mountains, deserts, and
" quicksands, since we went from home; and,
" after preaching the Gospel all over England
" and Wales for pure love, here they have taken
" us up for horse-stealing, only for riding
" a horse (that we found grazing by a wood-
" side) about a mile or two, when I was ready
" to perish with the ague."

" Why, my friend Jerry," (says Mr.
Powel) " I think you might as well have
" been in your own stall, repairing old shoes, as
" rambling about the country to reform the
" world: but I will answer for it, Jerry,
" neither you, nor Mr. Wildgoose, had any
" hand in stealing this horse."—" I find,
" then," says Mr. Aldworth, " Mr. Powel
" does really know these men. Appearances
" are by no means in their favour; but what
" can you say for them, Mr. Powel?"—
" Why," replies Mr. Powel, " I will be an-
" swerable for their honesty; and that neither
" of them is concerned in the fact of which
" they are accused."

" I do not dispute Mr. Powel's knowledge of
" the criminals," says young Newland; " but
" the

" the circumstances are so strong against them,
" that, I think, we have nothing to do but
" to make their Mittimus."

" Sir," replies Mr. Aldworth, " many an
" innocent man has been condemned and ex-
" ecuted upon circumstantial evidence; we
" cannot, therefore, be too cautious in this
" affair."

" I am not going to condemn or to try
" them" (rejoins Newland with some quick-
ness); " that is the Judge's business. I shall
" only commit them to a Gaol till the assizes;
" when, I hope, their innocence will appear
" to the gentlemen of the Jury."—Mr. Powel
observed, however, " that it would be a great
" hardship for innocent men to lie in Gaol
" for three months upon so slight a suspicion."
To which Newland answered, " that the Law
" did not consult the ease of individuals, but
" the good of the whole." Mr. Aldworth
was going to reply; when a great bustle at the
summer-house door interrupted him.

CHAP.

CHAP. XXIII.

The real Highwayman produced. Tugwell escapes
a Gaol, and gets a Dinner.

THE noise at the summer-house door was
occasioned by another party of the hue-
and-cry, who had gone a different way, that
morning, in pursuit of the robber, and had
actually taken the real culprit, who, having
left his horse by the river's side, where Wildgoose and his friend found him, had escaped
through the wood into a different road, where
these people had seized him, from his guilty
appearance; and had actually found upon him,
not only the exact sum of money, with two
Portugal pieces, to which the Farmer immediately swore, but also an old pocket-book,
containing a regular account between the
Farmer and his Landlord; which, with other
circumstances, appeared so evident, that the
Justices had nothing more to do, but to commit him without further examination.

Mr. Aldworth, having now turned over the
rest of this ragamuffin assembly to the care of
his Butler (who never suffered any one, that
came.

came about bufinefs, to leave the houfe without fome refrefhment), defired Mr. Powel to
conduct his two countrymen into a little
breakfaft-room, as he thought it in vain to afk
Wildgoofe, in his prefent trim, to go into the
parlour where his company had dined. But
Mr. Aldworth himfelf, after making an apology to his other friends, returned, attended
by a fervant with a napkin and tray, and fome
remains of a plentiful treat; which was no
unfavoury profpect to people in Wildgoofe's
and Tugwell's fituation.

When the two Pilgrims had now refrefhed
themfelves, and Mr. Powel had recounted moft
of the occurrences in the neighbourhood during their abfence; he began to perfuade them,
with all the rhetoric in his power, to return to
their refpective homes. Tugwell liftened with
great complacency to this exhortation : but
Wildgoofe, with a religious obftinacy, perfifted in his firft refolution; faid, " he was not
" at his own difpofal, but fhould fulfill the en-
" gagements he was under to his friends;"
though he did not think fit to explain to
Mr. Powel the particulars.

Mr. Aldworth, when he found that Wildgoofe's elopement was contrary to his mother's
approbation,

approbation, shook his head with a melancholy air, and said, "he heartily sympathized "with every parent in that situation: and "that he could not but join with Mr. "Powel in advising Mr. Wildgoose to re- "turn to his mother. As I have suffered "myself by the imprudence of an only son, "I would endeavour to rescue any parent from "the like distress; and, I flatter myself, that, "on my late journey to town, I was instru- "mental in restoring a young Lady to her "friends, who, from some unaccountable "whim, had eloped, entirely alone, in the "stage-coach to London, and by my earnest "persuasions prevailed on her to return, the "very next day, in the same stage, to her father: "and I cannot but intreat you, Sir, though "a stranger, to restore your distressed mother "to her tranquillity, by accompanying Mr. "Powel to your native place."

As the imprudence which Mr. Aldworth lamented in his son was the pursuing his own inclinations, and marrying a young woman with less fortune than Mr. Aldworth had destined him for: so the reader will probably guess, that the young Lady, whom he had re-

scued

scued from destruction, was no other than Miss Townsend; in whose story Mr. Wildgoose was so much interested.

Wildgoose's colour came immediately into his cheeks; and he could hardly forbear discovering the acquaintance he had with that young Lady, and also informing Mr. Aldworth of the accident that had frustrated his benevolent intentions; which, if Miss Townsend had been indifferent to him, he would most certainly have done: but, as the delicacy of his passion made him reserved in speaking of her, so his surprize passed off without being remarked by the company.

As the afternoon was now far advanced, Mr. Aldworth invited Wildgoose (with his fellow traveller) to take a bed there; and told Wildgoose, "that his Butler should "finish what the Barber had been prevented "from doing by the insolence of the hue-and-"cry."—Wildgoose thanked the old Squire for his civility; but, not feeling himself quite happy in Mr. Powel's company, and finding a stronger attraction towards Gloucester the nearer he approached to it, he chose to proceed on his journey.

Wildgoose, however, sent his dutiful respects to his mother; and Tugwell took an opportunity of whispering to Mr. Powel, " that he did not half like this vagabond way " of life; and wished the Spirit would give " Mr. Wildgoose leave to return home again. " But, Master," says he, " tell our Dorothy " we shall be no losers by it. And here, " Master, please to give her this crooked six- " pence for a token." Mr. Powel smiled at Jerry's instance of generosity; but advised him to carry it himself.

The young Magistrate, Mr. Newland, on his return to his company, had acquainted them with all the particulars of Wildgoose's story; which raised the curiosity of the Ladies: and, when they were informed of their marching off, they all ran to the window which looked towards the lawn, where the two Pilgrims passed in review before them.

Tugwell's spirits being quite elevated by his good cheer, he took the lead, in his short jerkin, his jelly-bag cap (which he had kept on since the morning), and his wallet on his shoulder; which, by a kind of instinct, he

secured

secured amidst all adventures; and which, like

"His oaken staff, which he could ne'er forsake,
"Hung half before, and half behind his back."

Mr. Wildgoose, however, exhibiting only that side of his face which had undergone the Barber's operation, made no despicable appearance; but raised a concern in the Ladies, that so handsome a young man should have taken so odd a turn, and travel about the country like a Scotch Pedlar.

CHAP. XXV.

Man of Rofs.

WHEN the two friends were got clear of Mr. Aldworth's premises, and were now alone in the road to Gloucester; whilst Mr. Wildgoose was wrapped in meditation, Tugwell interrupted him, by commenting upon the adventures of the day, and observed what a narrow escape they had had from being sent to gaol. He said, "he would take care how "he got on horse-back again, especially upon "other folk's horses. What a fine story our

N 2   "Parson

"Parson will have to carry home! that I and
"your Worſhip were taken up for horſe-
"ſtealing!"—"Ah! Jerry," replies Wildgoofe; "how often muſt I remind thee of the
"bleſſing promiſed to thoſe who are unjuſtly
"perſecuted? 'Happy are ye, when men ſhall
"ſay all manner of evil of you, falſely, for
"my name's ſake."—"Yes, yes, that is
"true," ſays Jerry; "but a man does not
"like to be counted a thief, for all that,
"when a body does not deſerve it. One's
"good name is one's livelihood; and I never
"was counted a night-walker, or a ſheep-
"ſtealer, before I kept company with your
"Worſhip (as I may ſay): and I had rather
"have been ducked in a horſe-pond, or
"pelted with cow-turd, than have had the
"diſgrace of ſuch a ſcandalous thing.

"But come, hang it! we did get a good
"dinner at the Squire's, *howſomever*; and I
"believe he is a very honeſt gentleman."

Thus Tugwell went on, grumbling and con-
ſoling himſelf alternately, without much converſation from his Maſter, 'till they came, towards the evening, to a tolerable public-houſe;
where they thought it beſt to repoſe themſelves,
after the fatigues and diſtreſſes of the paſt day.

The

The firſt thing Wildgooſe did was, by Tug-well's admonition, to finiſh what the Barber had begun; after which, according to his uſual cuſtom, he went to impart ſome ſpiritual exhortations to the family that received him. There was in the kitchen an old Gentleman-farmer, with locks as white as wool, and a face as red as a red-ſtreak: he was ſmoaking his pipe, and drinking cyder, with my Landlord. Wildgooſe, perceiving by his diſcourſe that he came from the neighbourhood of Roſs, in Herefordſhire, took that opportunity of making ſome enquiries after the famous Man of Roſs, ſo juſtly celebrated by Mr. Pope for his public ſpirit and unbounded generoſity. "What! old Kyrle!" ſays the Farmer; "yes, "I knew him well: he was an honeſt old "cock, and loved his pipe and a tankard of "cyder as well as the beſt of us."——"Well," ſays Mr. Wildgooſe, "if he uſed them with "moderation, there was no great harm in "either of them: and though a man may "endow hoſpitals without charity, and build "Churches without Religion; and though "I am afraid the Man of Roſs relied too much "upon his good works; yet he was certainly

N 3 "a very

" a very ufeful man, and a great benefactor
" to your country."

" Yes," fays the old Farmer; " he cer-
" tainly made good roads, and raifed caufeys,
" and brought conduits of water to the
" town: but it was not *all* at his own ex-
" pence; he made the country pay for it, by
" pretty handfome levies, and a tax upon the
" public."

Wildgoofe was not a little fhocked at the
malignity of the vulgar part of mankind, in
detracting from the merit of the moft heroic
characters, and bringing every one down, as
near as poffible, to their own level; which
feemed to be the principle on which this jolly
old fellow proceeded in his character of the
benevolent and worthy Man of Rofs.

CHAP.

CHAP. XXVI.

Foreſt of Dean.   Equality of Mankind.

AS Wildgooſe was impatient to proceed on
his journey to Gloucester, he had gone
early to bed, and awoke early in the morning.
But Tugwell having been thoroughly harraſſed
and fatigued the preceding day, it was not
in his maſter's power to rouſe him from his
bed till near eight o'clock; when, as ſoon as
Jerry had taken a ſhort breakfaſt (which he
made a conſcience of not omitting), they ſet
forwards on their journey.

Their road lay through the romantic Foreſt
of Dean; and the very name of a Foreſt filled
Tugwell's imagination with ideas of wild
beaſts, robbers, and out-laws: and, though
Jerry had no great matter to loſe, all the
ſtories which he had ever heard in the chimney-corner, or read in his penny-farthing
hiſtories, now occurred to his memory. But,
upon Wildgooſe's aſſuring him, " there was
" no danger to be apprehended now-a-days,
" either from wild beaſts, giants, or out-laws,"

they

they jogged on pretty peaceably all the fore part of the day ; and about dinner-time, coming to a fine tuft of oaks, upon a bank by the fide of a cryftal brook, the coolnefs of the fcene invited them to reft a little in the heat of the day, and to regale themfelves with the contents of Jerry's wallet, which Mr. Aldworth's Butler had liberally furnifhed with provifions the preceding day.

While they were thus employed, Jerry began to make comparifons between the different fituation of fome poor fellows whom they had juft paffed by (who, in the dog-days, were fweating at the forge belonging to a great iron-work in the Foreft), and the company which they had feen the day before at Mr. Aldworth's. Jerry obferved, " how hard it " was that fome people fhould be forced to " toil like flaves, whilft others lived in eafe " and plenty, and the fat of the land !"—— " Ah ! Jerry," fays Wildgoofe; " true " happinefs does not confift in meat and drink, " but in ' Peace and joy in the Holy Ghoft :' " and, I am convinced, there is not that " difference in the real enjoyment of men, " which you imagine. You only fee the out- " fide of the wealthier part of mankind ; " and

" and know nothing of the care and anxiety
" they suffer, which is frequently more in-
" supportable than any bodily labour which
" poor people undergo."

" 'Odsbobs!" says Tugwell; " if I had
" but as good a dinner every day, as I had
" yesterday at the Justice's, I would not
" value of a straw all the care and *bangciety*
" in the world."

" Well," replies Wildgoose; " but these
" distinctions amongst mankind are absolutely
" necessary; and, whilst men have the liberty
" of doing as they please, it cannot be
" otherwise."

" I suppose," continues Wildgoose, " you
" would have every body provided for alike;
" so that no one should be, either very rich, or
" very poor."— " Why," says Jerry, " me-
" thinks it is very hard, that one man should
" have five or six hundred pounds a-year,
" when another mayhap has not fifty."

" Well, then," (replies Wildgoose) " we
" will suppose, that you and I, Jerry, and all
" the people of our parish, and in the next
" parish, and in the next market-town, and
" so on, had each an hundred pounds a-year,
" and no more."—" Aye, that I should like

N 5.   " now,

" now, well enough."—" Well, then, but
" where should I get my shoes made?" says
Mr. Wildgoose.—" Troth, Master, you
" must even make them yourself; for I should
" work for nobody, but for myself and our
" Dorothy."— " Well," says Wildgoose,
" and where would you buy your leather?"—
" Why, of Mr. Jones, the Currier, at
" Evesham."— " Where would you get awls,
" hammers, and cutting-knives?"—" Why,
" from Birmingham."— " Very well; and
" where would you get your cloaths made?"—
" Oh! Isaac, our Taylor, should work for
" me; he is a very honest fellow."

" Ah! Jerry," says Mr. Wildgoose, " thou
" dost not consider, that all these people
" would be fully employed in working for
" themselves; so that, for all thy hundred
" a-year, thou must not only make thy own
" cloaths, but raise thy own corn, build
" thy own house, make thy own chairs and
" tables, thy own linen, stockings, shoes,
" and buckles; and, in short, either every
" man must work ten times harder than the
" poorest man now does, or, if he were idle
" or extravagant, those that were more frugal
" and industrious would again grow rich, and
" the

" the others poor : which ſhews the unavoid-
" able neceſſity of that inequality amongſt
" mankind, with which your complaint
" began."

" Odzookers ! Maſter, why, I do not
" know but it may be true enough, as you
" ſay ; and perhaps I may be as happy as
" Squire Pelican himſelf, though we brew
" nothing but ſmall beer : for, though the
" Squire can afford to get drunk every day in
" the week, yet he is laid up with the gout
" half the year ; and, thank God ! I have
" ſeldom any thing the matter with me, except
" the cramp now and then ; and that I can
" cure by a cramp ring made of hinge of old
" Coffins."

N 5 :   C H A P.

CHAP. XXVII.

Perils amongst false Brethren.

THE two Pilgrims having repofed themfelves for a confiderable time in the heat
of the day, it grew almoft dark before they approached the city of Gloucefter. Tugwell
again began to renew the fubject of thieves and
robbers; but, as his Mafter had before raillied
him for his cowardly apprehenfions, Jerry affected to talk of Highwaymen in a jocular
ftrain. He faid, "the clevereft book he ever
"met with was, The Exploits of Captain
"James Hind, who lived in Oliver's days;"
and though, to Jerry's furprize, his Mafter
had never heard of him, "he was born," he
faid, "but at Chipping-Norton. Did you
"never hear how he ferved the Parfon?" continues Jerry.— "Not I, indeed," fays Wildgoofe.— "It is a comical fancy enough," fays
Tugwell. "Captain Hind had juft robbed a
"gentleman of two hundred pounds; but,
"more company being juft behind, he thought
"they would purfue him: and fo, meeting
"a poor

" a poor Parfon, who was a little pot-valiant,
" the Captain pretended he himfelf was pur-
" fued by fome highwaymen, and defired the
" Parfon to take one of his piftols, and fire it
" in the face of the firft man he met; whilft
" Hind rode down to the next village, to get
" more help. And fo, in fhort, the Parfon
" did; but was taken by the gentleman, and
" had like to be hanged for it.

" Another time, the Captain was enchanted
" for three years by an old Hag. But the cle-
" vereft trick is what he ferved the old Mi-
" fer."—— " Well, well," fays Wildgoofe, " I
" fhall liften no longer to thy ftories: I do not
" wonder that fuch foolifh tales delighted thee
" in thy unregenerate ftate; but, I am afraid,
" this fort of nonfenfical books have brought
" many a poor wretch to the gallows; as they
" always intereft one in favour of their heroes,
" and reprefent vice in too agreeable a light."

The road now lay through a dark lane,
fhaded with elms: and, Wildgoofe being
equally happy in the thoughts of feeing Mifs
Townfend, and in beholding the flourifhing
ftate of his little Church, which he had planted
under the care of the Barber and Mrs. Sarfenet, they moved along with profound filence,
whon

when out leaps a man from the edge, and, with
a thundering oath, fnapped a piftol full in the
face of Tugwell, who happened to be fore-
moft, which, however, only flafhed in the pan.
Tugwell, though not deficient in courage, as
we have obferved, yet was extremely terrified
at the fight of fire-arms, to which he had not
been accuftomed. He, therefore, bawled out,
" Murder! Murder!" and, running back,
knocked Wildgoofe down, and himfelf tum-
bled, a—fe-over-head, foufe upon him. The
Footpad, holding the piftol to Tugwell's head,
bid him and his Mafter, " deliver their money,
" or they were dead men."——Wildgoofe, who
had more prefence of mind, begged him, " to
" take away his piftol, and he would give him
" money enough to relieve his prefent *neceffity*;
" as nothing, he obferved, but the *utmoft ne-*
" *ceffity* could poffibly drive a man to fuch
" defperate acts of violence."

As Wildgoofe was proceeding in his unfea-
fonable exhortation, the Robber, who knew
his voice, cries out, " God forgive me! Ma-
" fter Wildgoofe! Is it poffible, that I fhould
" be fo unfortunate, as to make my very firft
" attack upon you! Do not you know me?"
proceeds he.— " Who are you, then?" fays
Wildgoofe.

THE SPIRITUAL QUIXOTE. 293

Wildgoose. — " Ah ! Sir ! I am Tom Keen
" the Barber, where your Worship lodged at
" Gloucester."——The two Pilgrims now recovered from their fright, but not from their
surpize; and enquiring, " what could pof-
" fibly tempt him to hazard both his life and
" his foul, by robbing upon the highway?"—
" Oh ! Sir !" fays the Barber, " nothing but
" the moft urgent neceffity, as you rightly ob-
" ferve. You yourfelf, however, (without in-
" tending it) have been the principal caufe of
" bringing me to this diftrefs. My neighbour
" Fillpot, at the public-houfe, out of fpite,
" paid off a year and a half's rent, which I
" owed my Landlord, feized upon my goods,
" turned me out of my houfe; and now my
" wife, who has juft lain-in, is deftitute of
" the neceffaries for a woman in her condi-
" tion; and my children are, at this inftant,
" crying for bread."

" Well," fays Tugwell, " I pity any one
" that wants a meal of victuals. But, 'fblood !
" that is no reafon why you fhould take away
" my life, and fire a piftol in my face."—
" Ah !" cries the Barber, " you were in no
" danger of your life from my piftol; for you
" may fee (if it were light enough) that it is
                                    " nothing

" nothing but a piftol tinder-box, which I
" took out of Mr. Pafty's (the fat Prebend's)
" bed-room, who has made no ufe of it thefe
" ten years."

Wildgoofe then faid, " he was forry to find
" that any degree of neceffity could fuggeft
" to him this method of relieving his diftrefs:
" but, as his firft attempt had been provi-
" dentially made upon himfelf," Wildgoofe
obferved, " it would be attended with no ill
" confequences; and, as he had been the
" caufe of his calamity, he hoped it would
" be in his power, fome time or other, to
" make him fome amends for his temporal
" fufferings.— But he hoped no diftrefs
" would ever prevail upon the Barber to be
" guilty of fuch another defperate attempt
" to relieve it."

CHAP.

CHAP. XXVIII.

Gloucester.

AS this worthy Triumvirate were now
travelling amicably together towards
Gloucester, Wildgoose enquired, " how Mrs.
" Sarsenet went on ?"——The Barber replied,
" he did not know that her business declined
" at all; and Mrs. Sarsenet was a very good
" woman. But" (says he) " charity begins
" at home. She has got an old infirm mo-
" ther and a lame sister to support; and yet,
" she has of late so many spiritual Bargemen
" and pious Colliers, that come up from
" Bristol, whom she entertains at breakfast
" with tea and coffee, and buttered rolls, that,
" I am afraid, it is more than she can well
" afford.

" And then the young woman that lodged
" with her is gone away; and, I suppose,
" she paid handsomely for her board (for I
" find her father is a rich Squire); and she
" was a clever, notable young body, and of
" great use to her in her business."

This

This piece of news was a great difappointment to Mr. Wildgoofe; which, with the
fhock he received from hearing the ill confequences of his preaching (to the temporal
interefts of his difciples), threw him into a fit
of mufing, and put a ftop to their converfation
till they arrived at Gloucefter.

It was near ten o'clock when Wildgoofe
and his fellow-travellers reached the town.
Having, however, fupplied the poor Barber with
half a guinea for his immediate neceffities,
which was full as much as he could prudently
fpare out of his prefent ftock; he and Tugwell
went to Mrs. Sarfenet's, whom they found
at fupper, with her mother and fifter, upon a
bunch of radifhes and fome dry bread.

Mrs. Sarfenet was greatly rejoiced to fee
Mr. Wildgoofe, to whom fhe was a moft
fincere convert. She offered to get the travellers fomething for fupper, and alfo told
Wildgoofe, " that, as he was deprived of
" his old lodging, he fhould be welcome to
" the bed in which Mifs Townfend had lain."
Wildgoofe, though he probably thought
(what David faid of Goliab's fword), that
there was none like it; yet Mrs. Whitfield
(after fhe became acquainted with his merit
                                                when

when last at Gloucester) having pressed him to leave his lodgings at the Barber's, and come to the Bell; he now thought it would be very convenient, at least for that night, to accept of her kindness, and improve the favourable opinion which she seemed now to entertain of him.

Having made all proper enquiries, therefore, after Miss Townsend, and being informed of all the particulars — "that Mr. Townsend had "sent a carriage, and conveyed her to a re-"lation's in Warwickshire;" and having read three or four times over a direction, written with her own hand, "To Miss Julia Town-"send, at Dr. Greville's, at ———, near War-"wick;" he sighed, and took his leave of Mrs. Sarsenet for that evening, and went to Mrs. Whitfield's, at the Bell, to the no small joy of Tugwell; who infinitely preferred the smoak and savoury smell of a greasy kitchen to the meagre neatness of Mrs. Sarsenet's parlour, notwithstanding it was adorned with a glass-door, to peep into the shop, and the Ten Commandments, worked at the boarding-school, in a gilt frame; with King William and Queen Mary, and several other Metzo-
tintos

tintos painted on glafs, which had been in the family ever fince the Revolution.

CHAP. XXVIII.

The Pilgrims kindly treated by Mrs. Whitfield.

MRS. Whitfield received Mr. Wildgoofe with great cordiality, notwithftanding he brought no letters of recommendation from her brother-in-law, as the reader may fuppofe, on account of his precipitate departure from Briftol. Mrs. Whitfield's hufband, being fatigued with *too clofe attention* to the *proper bufinefs of* his calling, was retired to reft : fo that fhe was at fupper alone, upon a brace of partridges, with a large China *bafon* of warm punch ; which was no difagreeable contraft to the mortified repaft of poor Mrs. Sarfenet. And, as the relation fhe ftood in to Mr. Whitfield fanctified whatever fhe did in the eyes of Mr. Wildgoofe, he made no fcruple in partaking with her of the good things which were fet before him. Mrs. Whitfield laid Wildgoofe in one of her bettermoft rooms, the only good bed he had met with fince he came from home ;

home; and Tugwell alfo fhared the fame kindnefs: which made ample amends for the con-
tumelious reception they had met with on their
firft arrival at Gloucefter.

Though the little Church, which Wildgoofe
had planted, was partly diffolved by the poor
Barber's calamity; yet, the next morning, he
collected as many of the Brethren together as
could be fuddenly affembled, and gave the
word of exhortation to them in a field belonging to Mr. Whitfield at the Bell.

Before he departed, he recommended to them
the Barber's diftreffed condition; and, by confulting alfo with Mrs. Sarfenet and Mrs. Whitfield, they put him in a method of recovering
part of his old cuftomers; and Mrs. Whitfield
promifed to get him the occafional cuftom at
the Bell, as the Barber who ufed to attend
was going to fettle at Bath.

CHAP.

CHAP. XXIX.

Set out for the North.

THE two Pilgrims being now within a day's
journey, or a little more, of their native
place; Tugwell was impatient to return home,
partly to see his good wife Dorothy, and partly
to recount his adventures amongſt his neighbours, and exhibit the fancied improvements
he had made in his travels. Wildgooſe, indeed, was principally bent on purſuing the
great objeét which had taken peſſeſſion of his
imagination: yet the impreſſion, which Miſs
Townſend had made on his heart, a little di-
ſtraéted his thoughts, and made him deliberate,
whether he ſhould go the neareſt way into
Stafford and Shropſhire (which was through
Worceſter); or go round by Warwick, where
he had ſome proſpeét of ſeeing Miſs Townſend. As in the latter caſe, however, he could
not well avoid paſſing through his own village,
where he might meet with ſome obſtruétion
to his projeét from Mrs. Wildgooſe, he determined upon the former. Accordingly, after
taking

taking leave of his friends at Gloucefter, and writing a tender epiftle to Mifs Townfend, and exhorting Mrs. Sarfenet to join a little of the prudence of the ferpent with the innocence of the dove, Mr. Wildgoofe and his friend Tugwell fet out for Worcefter.

END OF THE SECOND VOLUME.

p. 2 - Tricks at an inn
p. 46 -
61, 67, 68. T— — boarder

Check Out More Titles From HardPress Classics Series In this collection we are offering thousands of classic and hard to find books. This series spans a vast array of subjects – so you are bound to find something of interest to enjoy reading and learning about.

Subjects:
Architecture
Art
Biography & Autobiography
Body, Mind &Spirit
Children & Young Adult
Dramas
Education
Fiction
History
Language Arts & Disciplines
Law
Literary Collections
Music
Poetry
Psychology
Science
…and many more.

Visit us at www.hardpress.net

Im The Story

personalised classic books

"Beautiful gift.. lovely finish.
My Niece loves it, so precious!"

Helen R Brumfieldon

⭐⭐⭐⭐⭐

UNIQUE
GIFT

FOR KIDS, PARTNERS
AND FRIENDS

Timeless books such as:

Kids

Alice in Wonderland · The Jungle Book · The Wonderful Wizard of Oz
Peter and Wendy · Robin Hood · The Prince and The Pauper
The Railway Children · Treasure Island · A Christmas Carol

Adults

Romeo and Juliet · Dracula

Highly
Customizable

Change
Books Title

Replace
Character Names
with yours

Upload
Photo to go
inside pages

Add
Inscriptions

Visit
Im The Story .com
and order yours today!

CPSIA information can be obtained
at www.ICGtesting.com
Printed in the USA
BVHW091902220819
556561BV00021B/4915/P